D1549874

This book is due for return on or before the last date shown below.

Why the Mind Is Not a Computer

A Pocket Lexicon of Neuromythology

Raymond Tallis

ia

IMPRINT ACADEMIC

Published in the UK by Imprint Academic
PO Box 200, Exeter EX5 5YX, UK

Published in the USA by Imprint Academic
Philosophy Documentation Center
PO Box 7147, Charlottesville, VA 22906-7147, USA

ISBN 0 907845 94 0

A CIP catalogue record for this book is available from the
British Library and US Library of Congress

Contents

Introduction

From the Theory of Meaning
to the Philosophy of Mind

In the last century, philosophy in the English-speaking world took a linguistic turn. This had two major manifestations: the radical claim that philosophy was primarily and essentially about the relationship between language and the world; and the less radical claim that many philosophical problems could be solved by paying attention to the way words were used in ordinary life — when they were not 'idling', as they seemed to be in much philosophical talk. One of the most conspicuous casualties of this approach was the epistemological project, which Descartes had identified as 'the first philosophy', and the Cartesian approach to the mind. Indeed, Frege was seen by his leading commentator, Michael Dummett, as the twentieth century's retort to Descartes: he overturned the Cartesian revolution that had elevated epistemology and the philosophy of mind to the status of 'the first philosophy' and put the philosophy of language and the theory of meaning in its place.[1]

For many people, the linguistic turn seemed eventually to reduce philosophy to a series of sterile exercises; though no-one actually reading the writings of, say, Gilbert Ryle or J.L. Austin — let alone less narrowly linguistic analytical philosophers such as W.V. Quine, P.F. Strawson or Saul Kripke — could avoid being amused, stimulated and challenged. The stigma of trivial-

---

[1]   See Michael Dummett 'Frege's Place in the History of Philosophy', the final chapter of his monumental *Frege: Philosophy of Language* (1973). For a sketch of the wider background of this revolution, see Tallis (1999a; 2005).

ity, however, stuck and in the case of many minor practitioners it was justified. Too many philosophers seemed satisfied with solving petty problems, and affirming semantic distinctions, of interest only to other philosphers. It was inevitable that, sooner or later, the kind of metaphysicalising that Frege and Wittgenstein had encouraged many philosophers to despise would return. By the end of the 1970s, as Simon Blackburn remarked, the philosophy of mind had displaced the philosophy of language as 'the queen of the philosophical sciences'.[2] Epistemology of a sort — a genetic rather than a justificatory epistemology — was back.

There were many specific reasons for this 'anti-linguistic turn'. It became increasingly obvious that a stand-alone theory of meaning was not possible. Frege's insistence that words had meaning only in the context of propositions or sentences — a point he used in order to attack a psychologism that tried to cash verbal meanings as mental images (and other contents of consciousness) associated with individual words — opened the door to the acknowledgement that, as Wittgenstein put it, 'propositions had meaning only in the stream of life'. When the theory of meaning was applied to natural languages — the ultimate target of any such theory — it had therefore to take account of things that had little to do with the rules governing the construction of well-formed formulae and for deriving one from another; indeed, things outside language narrowly construed. Austin's emphasis on speech *acts* also widened the scope of linguistic philosophy beyond the horizon of the Ordinary Language Philosophy particularly associated with his name. Philosophers such as H.P. Grice emphasised how speech depended upon speakers communicating their intentions and recipients understanding those intentions.

None of this of course would have come as a revelation to someone not trained in a philosophical tradition that hoped to tame natural languages by reducing them to formal features similar to those seen in mathematical systems. It was, however,

[2]   Blackburn (1986). This view of where philosophy is now has not been accepted by all, and there is certainly still much high-quality work being carried out in the philosophy of language a couple of decades on.

the death knell of the Fregean project of logicising language and, as a consequence of this, the dream of solving or dissolving philosophical problems by making philosophical discourse logically more transparent. The theory of meaning had to take account of the fact that meaning was something that people *meant* and other people had to understand as being meant. It was a matter of consciousness as well as of concepts. The consequences were spelt out by John Searle in his influential book *Intentionality*, published in 1983:

> A basic assumption behind my approach to the problems of language is that the philosophy of language is a branch of the philosophy of mind. (Searle, 1983, p.vii)

The thinking that lay behind this was, as we shall see, lost when the new philosophy of mind got underway.

The Analytical Heritage and the Aetiology of Neuromythology

When the theory of mind returned as a respectable preoccupation of philosophers it was a rather different activity from the metaphysicalising of the past. It was marked by habits of thought associated with the analytical tradition. At least two characteristics of analytical philosophy survived the collapse of what we might call the post-Fregean project. These were, first, a respect for science and, secondly, anti-psychologism or, more widely, a preference for a 'philosophy of concepts' over 'a philosophy of consciousness'. A third characteristic — an obsessive concern with appropriate use of language — did not, alas, carry over into the new philosophy of mind. Which is why this Lexicon has been necessary.

Respect for science is an indubitable part of the analytical heritage. This was a key aspect of the anti-metaphysical stance of leading figures in the Vienna Circle, whose influence, through the diaspora of the 1930s, was widespread and enduring. For some, the attitude to science went beyond simply accepting its findings — rather than challenging them with 'metaphysical' ideas dreamed up in armchairs or religious ones preached from pulpits — to thinking of philosophy as in important respects a commentary on, or unifier of, science. Many philosophers were also attracted by the model of science as a cooperative endeavour: progress in philosophical problems would be the result, not of the inspired guesswork of charismatic individuals of genius, but of the painstaking labours of many professionals working together. Austin commended 'Neither a be-all nor an end-all be' as a motto for philosophers.

Eventually, admiration for science and its methods modulated into something more subservient. Some thinkers began to agree with their more scornful scientific colleagues that in many areas of investigation philosophy was an anachronism. Philosophical investigations, after all, lacked sophisticated instrumentation: intuition-driven arguments, entangled with everyday prejudices, could hardly match the discovery procedures of science. The notion that philosophy was merely immature science particularly haunted the revived philosophy of mind. Quine's position that traditional epistemology was simply a rather primitive precursor of cognitive psychology seemed a depressing truth. Respect for the findings and critical attitudes of science modulated into what might be called 'science-cringe'.

'Science-cringe' was reinforced by dramatic developments in science itself. For the philosophy of mind, progress in the second half of the twentieth century in basic neurosciences — neuroanatomy, neurophysiology, neuropharmacology, neuropsychology, etc. — was of particular significance. These seemingly relevant sciences had apparently greatly enhanced their explanatory power by the acquisition of new techniques of exploring brain function (such as macroscopic and microscopic electrophysiology, immunology, imaging of the living brain) and new conceptual frameworks such as those derived from computer science. While philosophers might take pride in being anti-Cartesian, they felt increasingly uneasy about talking about the mind without reference to the sciences of the mind, if only because the latter were making such a big noise. While psychologism — the nineteenth-century doctrine that reduced logical entities, such as propositions, universals and numbers, to mental states or mental activities and subordinated much philosophy to branches of empirical psychology — was still decidedly off the menu, a philosophy of mind that took account of the findings of empirical neuroscience became increasingly respectable. Philosophers, moreover, were impressed by the arguments of U.T. Place, D.M. Armstrong and others in the 1950s and 1960s that the mind–brain identity theory — which justified the connexion between neuroscience and the philosophy of mind — need not be self-contradictory. The identification of mental events with neural ones could not be dismissed, it was argued, as a mere category error or a logical blunder.[3] What was more, those who led the reconceptualisation of mind from the direction of empirical science, such as Jerry Fodor, were philosophically sophisticated and brought with them an understanding of language that was highly formalised and, at the same time, rooted in both empirical psychology and neuroscience.

When the philosophy of mind resumed centre stage, therefore, it was a radically different enterprise from the one that had fallen into disrepute under the influence of post-Fregean philosophers such as Ryle, whose culminating, and seminal *The Concept of Mind* (1949) was mainly concerned with deflating or emptying its subject.[4] Increasingly, philosophers were inclined to accept Quine's famous assertion that 'Epistemology is best looked upon . . . as an enterprise within natural science'.[5] Those who want to understand the nature of knowledge, that most characteristic manifestation of the mind, should look to what scientists were discovering about cognition.

---

[3] There is a superb collection of essays celebrating this change in direction in C.V. Borst's *The Mind–Brain Identity Theory* (1970), which is now a brilliant record of how materialist theories of mind looked 35 years ago.

[4] This may be read as a rather loaded way of describing Ryle's contribution. A perhaps fairer description would be David J. Chalmers' assertion that Ryle codified 'the shift from the phenomenal to the psychological' aspects of consciousness (Chalmers, 1996, p. 14).

    As I shall discuss later, I am not entirely happy with this way of differentiating aspects of consciousness. It still seems to me that Ryle's approach to the mind beautifully illustrated Ernest Gellner's famous observation (directed at linguistic philosophy as a whole) that 'when a priest loses his faith, he is de-frocked; when a philosopher loses his, he re-defines his subject' (Gellner, 1959).

[5] Quine (1975), p. 68.

The capitulation to cognitive science is signalled in the final paragraphs of Avrum Stroll's superb historical essay on epistemology in the 1993 edition of the *Encyclopaedia Brittanica*:

> There have been explosive advances in neuroscience, psychology, cognitive science, neurobiology, artificial intelligence, and computer studies. These have resulted in a new understanding of how seeing works, how the mind forms representations of the external world, how information is stored and retrieved, and the ways in which calculations, decision procedures and intellectual processes resemble and differ from the operations of sophisticated computers, especially those capable of parallel processing.
>
> The implications for epistemology of these developments are equally exciting. They promise to give philosophers new understandings of the relationship between common sense and theorizing, that is, whether some form of materialism which eliminates reference to mental phenomena is true or whether the mental–physical dualism which common sense assumes is irreducible, and they also open new avenues for dealing with the classical problem of other minds. (Stroll, 1993)

The passage we have cited from John Searle earlier, in which he downgraded the philosophy of language to the status of a branch of the philosophy of mind, continues as follows:

> the capacity of speech acts to represent objects and states of affairs in the world is an extension of the more biologically fundamental capacities of the mind (or brain) to relate the organism to the world by way of such mental states as belief and desire, especially through action and perception. (Searle, 1983, p.viii)[6]

This indicates another route by which the philosophy of mind might cede authority to cognitive science: henceforth, philosophers should look to biologists for a definitive account of the nature of mind and its place in the order of things. All philosophers can do is provide a little conceptual assistance, putting in their penny's worth along with those working in adjacent fields such as linguistics and computational science.

---

[6] Searle has been consistent in his biologism. For example in his book *The Mystery of Consciousness*, he asserts that 'the correct approach' to consciousness is to keep reminding ourselves that the brain is a biological organ like any other, and consciousness is as much a biological process as digestion or photosynthesis (Searle, 1997, p. 163).

Not all philosophers of mind in recent decades have seen their roles as merely that of humble under-gardeners clearing the rubbish that clutters the way to neuroscientific truth. Scattered among the hordes of hard-line materialist neurophilosophers identifying the mind with neural activity and seeing epistemologists as neuroscientists' assistants and proselytisers are quite a few defiant dualists and 'mysterians' (*vide infra*). But neurophilosophy seems to be predominant and the mind–brain identity theory is now the default position in the philosophy of mind.

That it has achieved this ascendancy so rapidly is in part due to a second important influence of the analytical heritage on the revived philosophy of mind: resistance to taking seriously the reality of the phenomena of consciousness. The antipsychologism of Frege led, via the near-behaviourism of figures such as Wittgenstein and Ryle, to a wide-ranging suspicion of talk about memories, sensations, thoughts, beliefs and so on as if they were distinct, non-material, inner entities with an existence of their own. Anti-psychologism evolved into what we might call 'de-psychologism': an approach to psychology that tried to ignore, deny, or by-pass the subjective feelings of people who have minds. The origin of this aversion may well have been in part a longstanding muddle between a judgement as to the proper objects of philosophical inquiry (at least as construed by analytical philosophers) and a decision as to what actually exists.

This muddle may be seen at work in the impact of Gottlob Frege's massively influential essay 'The Thought'.[7] In this essay, he stipulates that:

---

[7]   Frege was not, of course, the only, or even the first, philosopher to try to reduce the mental activity of thought to the logical properties of symbolic systems in which thought might be expressed. Such attempts were perhaps anticipated in the title of George Boole's seminal book, in which he algebraicised logic: *An Investigation of the Laws of Thought on Which are Founded the Mathematical Theories of Logic and Probabilities* (1973). Frege, however, was most influential, not the least because of the advocacy of Bertrand Russell and, above all, of Wittgenstein, whose own influence was greatly magnified by his genius for metaphor and his charismatic and terrifying personality. It was through Frege that the project of mathematising logic and logicising mathematics inspired a wider antipsychologism.

> A property of thought will be called inessential which consists in, or follows from the fact that, it is apprehended by a thinker. (Frege, 1967, p. 37)

The essence of thoughts is not to be found in the experiences, or mental contents, of thinkers. These are incommunicable and have nothing to do with the communicable core that consitutes a thought. This has rather startling consequences; for example:

> [Thoughts] can be true without being apprehended by a thinker and are not wholly unreal even then. (p. 38)

This is not the place to discuss Frege's eccentricities.[8] Suffice it to say that the exclusive focus, in his 'inquiry' into thought, on thought-types that nobody has, rather than token thoughts that people have, exemplified the kind of thinking that seemed to justify what we might call 'de-psychologising' the mind. For Frege, the proper concern of philosophy was with the logical properties of thought and not with its psychology; with concepts rather than consciousness.

Even if one accepts the (dubious) assumption that the one can be addressed in the absence of the other, it does not follow that a purely logical inquiry can generate a satisfactory philosophical account of thought. Nevertheless, many philosophers found, and have continued to find, the example of this purely formal approach to thought (and, more widely, to the mind) compelling. Frege's influence — and that of his innumerable followers — is still evident in many areas of philosophy today: in 'minimalist' theories of truth that reduce the latter to its formal properties;[9] in 'thinly criterial' accounts of knowledge that empty it of subjective awareness[10] resulting in the absurdities exposed by 'Gettier examples' and the Frege-Gödel slingshot argument;[11] and in a resistance to acknowledging that propositional attitudes, such as beliefs and desire, as elements of consciousness,

---

[8]   Or some of the more interesting consequences of this counter-intuitive claim — such as the need to postulate a kind of sub-Platonic heaven where unthought thoughts can be stored, waiting for their moments of realisation. For a more detailed exposition and critique, see Tallis (2005), Section 1.3 'Depsychologising Thought'

[9]   Ibid Chapter 6 'Some Truths about Truth'

[10] Ibid Section 4.1 'What is Knowledge?'

[11] Ibid Section 6.2.4 'No Free Gifts'.

actually exist.[12] The most pervasive consequence of Fregean anti-psychologism, particularly associated with Wittgenstein, was the tendency to 'grammaticalise' problems in the philosophy of psychology, and to dismiss mysteries such as those of first-person being as pseudo-mysteries that are the result of being deceived by the grammar of language into believing in the existence of entities corresponding to terms such as 'I'.[13]

The most striking, and for our present concerns the most relevant, evidence of the continuing influence of the hostility in analytical philosophy to mental contents, is the vogue for theories of mind that evacuate the latter of contents of consciousness and/or equate them with linguistic or quasi-linguistic entities construed in an abstract, grammatical way. 'Syntactical theories of mind' that reduce the mind to sets of rules linking inputs and outputs in a functionally effective way[14] — offered as a 'scientific' alternative to the 'folk psychology' which invokes entities such as beliefs[15] — are only the most literal expressions of this ubiquitous influence. The prominence in this Lexicon of terms

---

[12] Ibid Section 5.5 'Propositional Attitudes'. In a fascinating interview, Michael Dummett, the pre-eminent interpreter of Frege for the English-speaking world, had this to say: ' The fundamental idea for Frege was that the contents of what are now called propositional attitudes — that is, things that are believed or known — which he called "thoughts", are not mental contents. They are not ingredients of the stream of consciousness. Such ingredients are things that are purely subjective: mental images, sensations, feelings, and so forth. By "thoughts" Frege means not particular acts of thinking but the contents of those acts; and these contents are objective, that is, common to all. One person can think, or consider, or deny just that very same thought which somebody else asserts. Frege made a sharp division between the subjective, which cannot be fully communicated, and the objective which, being independent of any particular mind must, Frege believed, exist independently of being grasped or thought about.' (Dummett in Pyle, 1991, p. 2)

[13] For a detailed critique of the 'philosophical grammar' approach to the 'I', see Tallis (2004), Chapter 2 '"Therefore I Am . . ." The Cogito Argument and the Bio-Logic of First-Person Identity'.

[14] See Tallis (1991/1999), pp. 116–19. Analytical philosophers do not always recognise their own progeny. In his autobiography, *The Making of a Philosopher* (2003), Colin McGinn describes the reaction of Michael Dummett to a talk McGinn gave on the Syntactic Theory of Mind. Dummett launched into a violent attack on McGinn's paper that betrayed his ignorance of the both the context and provenance of McGinn's argument.

[15] See especially Stich (1983) and Churchland (1994).

such as 'calculation', 'grammar', 'logic', 'rule' testifies to the after-life of Fregean ways of thought in the philosophy of mind. Only after 'the linguistic turn' could philosophers be inclined to think of the mind as an ensemble of 'symbol processing devices', a 'syntactic engine operating on mental sentences' and the like.

The influence of analytical thought on the philosophy of mind is strikingly illustrated in the writings of Daniel Dennett (whose teacher at Oxford was Gilbert Ryle). Dennett combines a Rylean disdain for the contents of consciousness with a tendency to speak of processes in the brain in (consciousness-free) linguistic terms. This approach was also clearly illustrated by Patricia Churchland in her landmark publication *Neurophilosophy. Towards a Unified Theory of the Mind/Brain*. 'Nervous systems', she claimed, 'are information processing systems'.[16] With something bordering on bet-hedge, however, she noted, several hundred pages later, that 'Only in a *very* abstract sense is the brain like a computer'.[17] In between she gives much sympathetic coverage to the notion of mental activity and cognition as 'sentence-crunching'. Without entirely committing herself, she offered house-room to Fodor's until recently hugely influential idea that the tissues of the mind are composed of symbols, and that intelligent behaviour is informed by a language of thought called 'mentalese'. She claimed that 'propositions and the logical relations defined over them constitute an impressively powerful structure':

> It is this insight, made more appealing by the discoveries of modern logic and by the construction of electronic devices conforming to logic, that has engendered a certain 'logicist' conception of the mind. On this conception, the mind is fundamentally a sentential computing device, taking sentences as input from sensory transducers, performing logical operations on them, and issuing other sentences as output. (p. 305)

The mind, in short, is a device that is in the business of carrying out up-to-date, post-Fregean logical operations. By representing the mind in this way, the analytical preference for concepts over consciousness could be preserved and the revival of the philosophy of mind would seem to be less of a return to

[16] Churchland (1986), p. 36.
[17] Ibid. p. 408.

discredited Cartesian preoccupations. (The fact that neuroscientific accounts of the mind were overwhelmingly anti-dualist also helped.)

The syntactic theory of mind has seemed to be a little empty even to the most committed logicisers of human consciousness. While Dennett has insisted that 'the brain is a syntactic engine, not a semantic machine'[18] most other (conscious and unconscious) post-Fregeans want to grant the language of the mind semantics as well as syntax. There seemed little point in processing symbols if those symbols symbolised nothing. This was, of course, the point of Searle's famous Chinese Room thought experiment which triggered many famous spats, not the least with Dennett himself.[19] Even languages, after all, have semantics as well as syntax. For some neurophilosophers, this was provided by the causal relationships between the input and output of the nervous system: the material world that the meat-mired mind was wired into.

The lengths that post-analytical philosophers of mind have gone to in order to avoid acknowledging contents of consciousness have been extraordinary. Dennett, however, remains the doyen of consciousness-deniers because, it seems, that for him science has the last word. There are third-person phenomena accessible to science as he narrowly construes it — 'stimulus inputs', 'reactive dispositions' and 'discriminative states' — but no 'inner feelings'.[20] Neurophilosophers have made it a matter of honour even to deny the existence of such things as beliefs, desires, and so on.[21] These 'propositional attitudes' are imaginary entities postulated in folk psychology to make sense of the surprising, but comprehensible, behaviour of our fellow organisms; unnecessary middle terms in the functional links between sensory input and behavioural output. And as for 'selves', they are fictions — rather Byzantine fictions; according to Dennett,

[18]   Dennett (1981).
[19]   Nicely encapsulated in Searle's review of Daniel Dennett's *Consciousness Explained* (1991) for *The New York Review of Books* and the bracing exchange that followed. It is all in Searle (1997).
[20]   These topsy-turvy views can be found in Dennett (1991).
[21]   See Stich (1983) and Churchland (1986; 1994).

the self is a 'Center of Narrative Gravity' and 'all the phenomena of human consciousness are explicable as "just" the activities of a virtual machine realized in the astronomically adjustable connections of a human brain'.[22] Qualia are difficult, propositional attitudes are difficult, selves are difficult, so away they must go: they cannot be accommodated in the third-person neurophilosophical framework that combines scientism with an analytical outlook that prefers concepts to consciousness, placing consciousness-free language at the heart of the human mind.[23]

While it would be both implausible and historically inaccurate to suggest that neurophilosophy is solely the child of post-Fregean anti-psychologism, it seems likely that this deeply counter-intuitive kind of thinking would have had a much harder time being accepted if it had not been for background assumptions of analytically trained philosophers who had hoped to trump the philosophy of mind and knowledge with a theory of meaning; and who had become accustomed to disregarding (incommunicable) subjective consciousness in favour of a propositional calculus and a philosophical grammar that aimed to explain how language connected with the world. Had it not been, in short, for a philosophical outlook that abbhored dealing with mental phenomena as if they were irreducibly real entities in their own right.

The most commendable feature of analytical philosophy was, of course, commitment to extreme care in the use of terms. This was rooted in the suspicion that many, perhaps most, of The Big Problems in philosophy arose when, as Wittgenstein put it, language went 'on holiday'. Unfortunately, this part of the heritage — possibly the one which has most enduring value — seems to have been jettisoned when the philosophy of mind returned in a neurophilosophical guise. As the intense suspicion of linguistic philosophers towards traditional epistemological concerns gave place to an uncritical acceptance of neuroscience, and the theory of knowledge was ingested into neuro-epistemology, obsessive concern with the need to use terms correctly was replaced by a

---

[22] Dennett (1991), p. 410
[23] See Tallis (1991/1999).

rather passive assimilation of the language and linguistic habits of non-philosophical disciplines apparently most relevant to the philosophy of mind.

I am referring to 'the language of neuromythology' that is the theme of the present Lexicon.

Myth-Information

This booklet was first published a decade ago and the problem that it identified has not gone away. Things have, if anything, got worse: thinking by transferred epithet; sneaking across the mind–brain barrier using, as cover, terms that have roots in both mental and physical domains; machinising the mind; anthropomorphising and machinising the brain and bits of the brain; attributing to isolated brains — or neural ensembles or even single synapses — properties, qualities and faculties that whole persons in entire worlds would be proud to possess; succumbing to the fallacy of misplaced explicitness — all of these intellectual follies have spread in the intervening ten years from a philosophical epidemic to a near-pandemic. One example of the continuing relevance of this Lexicon will have to suffice.

In the Lexicon, I identify 'Information' as 'the big one':

> an absolutely key term in cognitive science and much contemporary thought about brain function, the mind and the relationship between them. (p. 54, below)

It has been a key term because neurophilosophers speak both of events not associated with consciousness and of contents of consciousness as pieces of information. In the entry on this term, I ended by arguing that:

> Once the concept of information is liberated from the idea of *someone being informed* and from that of *someone doing the informing*, anything is possible. (p. 69, below)

I could almost have been predicting David Chalmers' extraordinary *The Conscious Mind: In Search of a Fundamental Theory* which caused such a stir among neurophilosophers in the late 1990s.[24]

---

[24] Chalmers (1996). The jacket carried encomia from Colin McGinn, Steven Pinker and — most surprisingly — David Lewis, one of the founding

Chalmers' book was welcomed because it did not try to duck 'the hard problems' by pretending that the contents of consciousness — awkward things like qualia, subjective feelings, and the like — did not really exist. Chalmers accepts that they do exist. Indeed, he divides those aspects of the mind which can be analysed functionally and seemto be amenable to the current neuro- philosophical approaches or, more widely, to be proper objects of cognitive science, from those which cannot and are not. The former are 'psychological aspects'[25] and are connected with the mind's role in bringing about behaviour — its function as a way-station between environmental inputs and behaviour outputs — while the latter are phenomenal properties, which are 'conscious experience of mental states'. The challenge, which neurophilosophers cannot escape and cannot meet within their current conceptual framework, is to account for 'the varieties of conscious experience'; to explain how, given that the brain is in the last analysis simply a lump of matter, admittedly one with rather special properties, such experiences arise.

Chalmers' explanation is that consciousness arises in virtue of 'the functional organisation of the brain' (p. 247) which is 'best understood as *the abstract pattern of causal interaction* between various parts of a system' (p. 247). In the Lexicon, I make clear (I think) why one cannot appeal to patterns, let alone abstract ones, to underpin consciousness.[26] My main interest here is in what happens next; in particular where his arguments take him and the unbridled speculations that attracted such attention

---

fathers of consciousness-empyting functionalism. Lewis described it as 'the best book in philosophy of mind for many years'. Certainly, it is beautifully written, a scholarly and thoughtful book. The best possible account of the state of the art — and of the mess it is in. Unfortunately, it is part of the mess.

[25] A usage which Chalmers acknowledges as a 'stipulation', that arises from 'identifying psychology with cognitive science' (p. 12). He admits that 'the everyday concept of a "psychological state" is probably broader than this'. You bet.

[26] See the entries below on 'Pattern' and also 'Level'. Chalmers is very dependent upon the notion that 'the relevant sort of functional organisation' will always be at a level 'fine enough to determine behavioural capacities', while recognising that the brain can be viewed at coarse as well as fine-grained levels — for example as a 'two-component organisation' made up of two hemispheres' (p. 247).

from the neurophilosophical community.[27] By identifying consciousness as the product of 'fine-grained functional organization' he is obliged to accept that anything that has such a
functional organisation will have consciousness. This is because
the link between functional organization and consciousness is
'information': information 'is the key to the link between physical processes and conscious experiences' (p. 287).

This may seem counter-intuitive to anyone who thinks of the
transmission or receipt of information as a sophisticated product of consciousness rather than its physical basis. He neutral-
ises this by mobilising a generous definition of what counts as
'information'. 'Information', he argues, appealing to a slogan
from Gregory Bateson 'is a difference that makes a difference'.
(p. 281). This licenses him to conclude that devices such as
thermostats, which are 'information processing devices', are
conscious.

The slippery slope envisaged in the entry on 'Information' in
this Lexicon is now embarked upon. Since what goes on in a
thermostat is not fundamentally different from what goes on
elsewhere in the universe — except insofar as thermostats are
designed to regulate our environments according to our wishes
— we may extend the notion of information and experience:

> If there is experience associated with thermostats, there is prob-
> ably experience *everywhere*: wherever there is causal interaction,
> there is information, and wherever there is information there is
> experience. One can find information states in a rock — when it
> expands and contracts, for example — or even in the different
> states of an electron. So there will be experience associated with
> a rock or an electron. (Chalmers, 1996, p. 297)

Thermostats may not have the capacity to introspect or think, or
be blessed with self-consciousness (p. 295) but they may have
beliefs and desires (p. 388). In Chalmers' vision, it seems, the
entire universe becomes rather gossippy, a massive auto-
pandiculation, a global bean-spilling; and rocks are rather less

---

[27]   And earned him such harsh criticism from John Searle in his review in *The
New York Review of Books* (reprinted in Searle, 1997). This review is justly
hard on the speculations but does not, I think, adequately acknowledge the
brilliance of the early chapters of Chalmers' book and its critique of
standard neurophilosophy.

numb than their brutish exterior might suggest to the philosophically uninformed. Since rocks are conscious, there cannot of
course, be any reason for denying that the brain should be conscious. Why, after all, should it be *under*privileged in this crucial
respect compared with electrons?

Chalmers' book shows how close hard-headed computational
cerebro-centric thinking about the human mind lies to super-
soft pan-psychism. The language of neuromythology — in
which the brain is both machinised and anthropomorphised —
should warn us that just beneath the rhetoric of tough-minded,
materialist scientism is magic thinking: thoughts in thing-like
brains open the way to 'mind among things'. More specifically,
it shows how, once you use a Janus-faced term like 'information'
to make consciousness seem less special, the latter has a tendency to spread all over the place. The penalty of subscribing to
the Fallacy of Misplaced Consciousness — attributing consciousness to neurones, for example, or claiming that things like
retinas do things like calculations — is that consciousness will
pop up everywhere; even (for those who are consistent and have
the courage of their convictions) in rocks and electrons.[28]

More specifically still, it shows that if the mind–matter problem shrinks to the mind–body problem, and the mind–body
problem shrinks to the mind–brain problem, and mind is eventually straitjacketed so that we have the mind–bits-of-brain
problem, such tension will build up that, eventually, there will
be an explosion scattering mind over the entire universe.
Chalmers' speculations may seem aberrant but they are the
absurdity to which neurophilosophical ideas are constitution-
ally liable to be reduced. If Chalmers has a fault, it is in his

---

[28] Chalmers' panpsychism denies him one of the other favourite explain-alls
of neurophilosophers — localisation. The notion that the emergence of
consciousness, and its differentiation into qualitatively different conscious
experiences, can be explained by the fact that the brain has more than one
part provides one of the most compelling sources of pseudo-explanations
in neurophilosophy. It creates new problems, of course. Keeping things
tidily apart only exacerbates the problem of bringing them together in a
unified consciousness. See Tallis (2005), Section 2.2.3 'The Unity of
Consciousness'.

remorselessness in uncovering the logical consequences of the premises from which neurophilosophy starts.

The assimilation of the mind to matter can also rebound in another way. Donald Davidson, as a way of encouraging people to fret less over physicalist theories of the mind, argued that there is 'no good reason for calling all identity theories "materialist"':

> if some material events are physical events, this makes them no more physical than mental. Identity is a symmetrical relation. (Davidson, 1987)

Materialising the mind is not, in the end, different from mentalising matter. Which is, perhaps, the hardest lesson neurophilosophers have yet to learn: they are not so tough-minded as they they think they are. They will not learn it so long as they are bewitched by their own terminology.

Neurophilosophy and Scientism

The language of neuromythology very effectively conceals the deficiencies in neural accounts of consciousness. I have written about these extensively elsewhere.[29] Quite apart from its inability to explain 'ground floor' sentience, and rudimentary contents of consciousness such as qualia, there is as yet no remotely plausible neurophilosophical account of, for example:

(a) the intentionality of perceptions and thoughts;

(b) their (ineliminable) indexicality;

(c) the unity of consciousness; and

(d) the architecture of everyday awareness.

In short, neurophilosophy cannot accommodate those things that make human beings distinctively human.

The notion of human beings as more or less independent points of departure, as selves reponsible for their actions, is simply incomprehensible if everything that makes up the self, the agent, is regarded as being identical with certain activity in the brain. Reasons, thoughts, purposes, intentions and so on

---

[29] Most recently in Tallis (2005), Chapter 2. However, there are more detailed discussions of the deficiencies of neural theories of mind in Tallis (1991; 1999b) and especially Tallis (2000), which covers the historical aspects.

become incorporated into causal chains that simply pass through neural tissue — linking sensory input with motor output — and out the other side. Thoughts and reason-led behaviour, just as much as sensations and twitches, are embedded in the material world and not under the control of a self as agent.

Sincere neurophilosophising obliges one to think as the preeminent neurophysiologist Colin Blakemore does in this passage:

> All our actions are products of the activity of our brains. It seems to me to make no sense (in scientific terms) to try to distinguish sharply between acts that result from conscious intention and those that result from our reflexes or are caused by disease or damage to the brain. (Blakemore, 1990, p. 270)

> We feel ourselves usually to be in control of our actions, but that feeling is itself a product of our brain, whose machinery has been designed, on the basis of its functional utility, by means of natural selection. (p. 270)

> To choose a spouse, a job, a religious creed — or even to choose to rob a bank — is the peak of a causal chain that runs back to the origin of life and down to the nature of atoms and molecules. (p. 272)

This, at least, has the virtue of honesty: neurophilosophy offers us no grounds for distinguishing between having an epileptic fit, consulting one's doctor about the fit, and writing a paper on the management of epilepsy.

This is no more radical than the views of an early neurophilosopher and Darwinian, the great physicist Ernst Mach, who argued that conditioned reflexes were 'rudimentary concepts' and that

> there is no difference between ordinary experience accessible to any being endowed with a nervous system and scientifically organised experiment. There is no break in continuity between science . . . and modes of behaviour characteristic of the entire animal world. (Kolakowski, 1972, pp. 146–7)

For some, far from being a weakness, this is a strength of neural theories of consciousness. Towards the end of her beautifully illustrated popular account of modern neuroscience *Maps of the Mind*, Rita Carter argues that, thanks to neuroscience, we are at last able to see the truth about ourselves:

> At the moment our legal and moral code is founded on the
> assumption that each of us contains an independent 'I' — the
> ghost in the machine that controls our actions . . . But now that
> the black box has been opened — [in other words we are able to
> look inside the living brain] [this view] is not easy to sustain . . .
> we see that actions follow from our perceptions and our percep-
> tions are constructed by brain activity . . . our actions are entirely
> mechanistic . . . (Carter, 1998, p. 206)

Of course, we believe that we are free, but this is an illusion,
albeit a stubborn one. It is

> deeply ingrained because it prevents us from falling into a sui-
> cidally fatalistic state of mind . . . it is one of the brain's most
> powerful aids to survival . . . Future generations will take for
> granted that we are programmable machines just as we take for
> granted the fact that the earth is round. (p. 207)

Carter's and Blakemore's views fit very snugly with the
immensely popular notions of the evolutionary psychologists
who argue that neural activity is structured to ensure that
behavioural outputs are linked to sensory inputs in such a way
as to maximise the chances of our finding nutrition and protect-
ing our young and minimising the chances of our being
destroyed by some hostile biological or non-biological element.
Unknown to ourselves, we are the playthings of our selfish
genes.

The general pattern of such arguments is that, if neural theories of consciousness cannot explain, or even accommodate, certain phenomena that we associate specifically with human
beings — such as leading more-or-less free, more-or-less self-
directed, lives — then those phenomena are illusory. If, to reiter-
ate Blakemore, it 'makes no sense (in scientific terms) to try to
distinguish sharply between acts that result from conscious
attention and those that result from our reflexes or are caused by
disease or damage to the brain', then those differences are
unreal. It could be argued with equal logic, however, that if neural theories of consciousness cannot account for, or even accept
the reality of, these things, then the theories are deficient: they do
not tell the whole story. The assumption that 'if science can't see
it, then it is isn't real' has nothing to do with science and everything to do with 'scientism' — belief in the 'omnicompetence of

science';[30] more precisely, in the omnicompetence of a sub-set of sciences — the natural, rather than the social, sciences.

Most people who espouse scientistic accounts of humanity seem to behave no differently from others who feel that the biological story of the human organism is not the end of the matter. So perhaps we should not take what they say too seriously. On the other hand, perhaps we should. For scientism has had dire effects in the twentieth century.

As Tzvetan Todorov (among others) has compellingly argued, the application of scientistic thought to human affairs has been one of the main motors of, and justifications for, totalitarian politics. Scientism — which, Todorov points out, 'is not science but a world-view that grew funguslike on the trunk of science' [31] — gave a scientific gloss to the classification of Jews as subhuman in Nazi Germany and the reduction of the Kulaks to 'objective class enemies' in Soviet Russia. In both cases, their status as human beings, as persons, as independent points of departure, was denied on quasi-scientific grounds. Individuality was subsumed under biological destiny on the one hand and historical inevitability on the other. To see people as machines — genetically determined or programmable — is no light matter.

While it is probably only in societies that are sick for other reasons that scientistic ways of thinking about humans are anything other than intellectual postures, and are used to justify wickedness, there is another reason for challenging them: they are wrong. Neurophilosophy is simply wrong about human beings and their place in — and outside of — nature. And because of this, they are certainly boring, even if their misrepresentation of humanity is not dangerous.

Towards a Critical Neuro-Epistemology

It is easy to mock the linguistic and other fudges necessary to make neural sense of human beings. It is less easy, having done so, to know what to make of those undeniable facts that neuro-

---

[30]   A phrase I have lifted from Mary Midgley's excellent *Science and Poetry* (2002).
[31]   Todorov (2004), p. 21.

science serves up to us, regarding the central role of the brain in our conscious lives. As a practising doctor treating patients with conditions such as stroke, Parkinson's disease, epilepsy and Alzheimer's disease, and as a clinical scientist whose central research interest is in diseases of the brain, I am acutely aware of the dependency of what we experience, think, feel and do on the functioning of our brains.

There is, for example, a clear relationship between brain damage — its extent and its location — and deficits in what are usually called 'higher mental function'. Even more striking than these negative observations are positive observations: the association between brain activity and experiences, as in the brain stimulation experiments of Penfield in waking human subjects undergoing epilepsy surgery; or, more mundanely, the complex hallucinations experienced by patients having complex partial seizures due to abnormal, spontaneous electrical discharges within the cerebral cortex. The recent advent of brain mapping, using powerful methods of imaging the activity of the living brain — functional magnetic resonance, topographical electro-encephalography, transcranial magnetic stimulation — has shown exquisite correlations between the quantity and location of neural activity and the level and, apparently, the contents, of consciousness.

Of course, one should not be over-impressed by the glamour of neuroscience. Far from being a recent understanding arising out of neuroscience, the central role of the brain in human consciousness, was stated very firmly by Hippocrates in the fifth century BC:

> Men ought to know that from the brain, and from the brain only, arise our pleasure, joys, laughter and jests, as well as our sorrows, pains, grief and tears. Through it, in particular, we think, see, hear, and distinguish the ugly from the beautiful, the bad from the good, the pleasant from the unpleasant. (Quoted in: Spillane, 1981)

That this idea was old even in Hippocrates' time was hardly surprising. Everyday observations, since the first caveman noted that his friend behaved oddly after being hit on the head with a rock, support the idea that the brain has a central role in sustaining ordinary consciousness. The effect of moving one's head, or re-directing one's eyes, or opening one's eyelids, on the contents of consciousness — experiments that require no Medical Research Council funding — seem to be most readily explained by the notion that sense organs such as the eyes are channels through which energy from the visible world impinges on, and activates, the brain and that this is the basis of vision.

We therefore have an interesting situation: neurophilosophy has serious problems explaining pretty well everything about human consciousness; and yet anti-neurophilosophy has its troubles too, in making sense of the undoubted role of the brain in supporting ordinary consciousness.[32] One response to the dilemma is to walk away from it and declare the mind–body problem a mystery which, due to the way our minds are constructed, we shall never solve. This approach, particularly associated with Colin McGinn[33] (dubbed 'mysterian' by Owen Flanagan)[34] is deeply unattractive. There is little point in doing philosophy if one is not interested in trying to make coherent sense of things, bringing together disparate, and even contradictory, observations. To quote Wilfred Sellars, one of the fundamental tasks of philosophy is to try 'To say how things, in the widest sense of "things" hang together, in the widest sense of "hang together"'.[35] What is more, genuine philosophical problems, such as the mind–body problem, are far too precious to be discarded; they are, after all, a way of grasping hold of ourselves. Almost as unattractive is the much-repeated idea (a version of the dual-aspect theory) that neural accounts of human consciousness and behaviour and everyday accounts are simply two ways of describing the same phenomena; that the attempt to reduce one to the other is misguided; and that we should simply

---

[32] For a more detailed account, see Tallis (2005), Section 2.3 'The Trouble with Anti-neurophilosophy'.
[33] See McGinn (1989).
[34] See McGinn (2003), p. 183.
[35] Quoted by Hilary Putnam in Pyle (1991), p. 52.

accept that different ways of describing things suit different purposes.[36]

A third approach is to claim, as I have done on several occa-
sions, that appropriate neural activity in a normally functioning
nervous system is a necessary but not a sufficient condition of
ordinary human consciousness and behaviour.[37] This would fit
with the observation that what we are and what we do are the
more readily understood in neural terms *the less well our brains
are functioning*. To put this another way, the more severely our
brains dysfunction, the closer our behaviour is to the direct
expression of cerebral activity. It is easier to give a fairly complete account of, say, an epileptic fit in terms of neural activity[38]
than to give an account of the patient's decision, after the fit is
over, to seek medical advice. Brain discharges may explain epileptic fits but not the behaviour of the citizen who is prone to
them when he is not suffering their effects. The brain is a necessary, but not a sufficient, condition of the latter.

I am not, of course, the first person to make this suggestion.
Merleau-Ponty, who of all the great twentieth century philosophers was most versed in contemporary neuroscience, made a
very similar point:

> Being a conscious subject is engaging in complex relations with
> objects, and these relations depend on the whole human being,
> not simply on the brain; a disembodied brain could not be said
> to have conscious experience of objects, but only to provide

---

[36]   While there is less talk nowadays of 'category errors' and other relics of
       the era of linguistic philosophy, it is obvious that the problem-dissolving
       or problem-denying attitude is part of the legacy of later analytical
       philosophy.

[37]   See Tallis (1999a,b).

[38]   Even then, the account would incomplete. Many people who have seizures
       make complex sense of them, which cannot be explained in neural terms.
       What is more, the reality of the hallucinations experienced during seizures
       is parasitical on the reality of the objects of normal experience. A brain in a
       vat (invoked in the well-known thought experiment of Hilary Putnam)
       would not formulate the idea of an external world because it would have
       no bodily relationship to real objects. It would have no real experiences to
       parasitise to justify, or motivate, the leap to objects. Even Wilder Penfield's
       subjects, who experienced full-blown, Proustian, memories when their
       brains were stimulated during epilepsy surgery, would not have had such
       memories had they not had many years of normal experiences and normal
       memories as persons living in worlds.

some of the necessary, but not sufficient, conditions for such conscious experiences. (Matthews, 2002, p. 57)[39]

This is not, however, any kind of explanation of the role of the brain. Nor does it point the way out of the paradox that, while neural activity fails to explain human consciousness, human consciousness is unthinkable without neural activity. It is, however, the framework within which an understanding of human consciousness — and, more widely, of the relationship between human being and the human organism, and hence the place of human beings in, and outside of, nature — must be sought.

Such understanding will not be arrived at if there is premature conceptual closure; if, under the influence of the language of neuromythology, we are misled into believing we know, and make coherent sense of, more than we in fact do. There is a huge challenge to be met, and the possibility of a fascinating intellectual journey, if we do not cheat in our attempts to link, say, human beings as citizens with the activity of their brains by importing, or reading back, the most sophisticated activities of citizens — 'calculations', 'information processing', etc. — into our descriptions of neuronal activity.

If we use up all the higher order language to describe neural activity — which in the last analysis is merely biophysical — we shall have nothing left over with which to capture the difference between neural activity and, say, people, who do complex things like making calculations. We shall be left either denying that there is such a difference (as we have seen many philosophers do); or simply despairing of connecting neural activity with the kinds of creatures we are and the complex ways in which we are aware of, and interact with, the world. We shall, in short, be forced into being either reductionists, who cannot account for our sense of self and our free will or for their undoubted significance, or into being mysterians, boringly reiterating *ignoramus et ignorabimus*.

---

[39] The idea that an isolated brain could sustain the kinds of experiences humans have is absurd. What would it have experiences about? Experience goes beyond the brain in two directions: to the entire engaged organism; and to society, history and the self.

There is a fascinating investigation to be undertaken into the connexions between the ground-floor, necessary conditions of human consciousness with the persons that we are. Before we can begin this investigation, we must acknowledge that the same kind of story cannot explain why my arm twitches when I have an epileptic fit and why I raised my arm the other day to make a point in response to a lecture about epilepsy. The former story will be largely entirely intracerebral; the latter will have to look beyond neural activity (which is asocial) to frames of reference that have no neurophysiological correlates. The story of how our human consciousness came to be through-and-through socialised, and of what we do with our profoundly socialised (and personalised) awareness, will not be exclusively, or even mainly, a biological story about brains or even about the evolution of brains to favour cooperative activity.

The saga of the explicit collectivisation of consciousness of human beings — who are, when well, least confined to their status as organisms (so that their agenda is least, or least directly, that of an organism) — and of their evolving selfhood and freedom is extraordinarily long, rich and complex. I have tried to sketch some of its most general features in a trilogy of books.[40] This trilogy, notwithstanding its total of over 1,000 pages, hardly begins to describe the distances between human beings and their neural activity, or to account for the progressive extension of those distances in the growth of the self, the expansion of freedom, and the widening of knowledge.

A huge task remains of making humanity *visible*. It would be an intellectual tragedy of the first magnitude if the language of neuromythology were to prevent us from seeing what humans have become and we were robbed of a great adventure of self-understanding that acknowledged not only the fact that we are a part of nature but that, in many various ways, we are apart from it. For that we need a *critical neuro-epistemology* that denies neither the reality of the mechanisms that operate in our bodies

---

[40] *The Hand: A Philosophical Inquiry into Human Being* (2003), *I Am: A Philosophical Inquiry into First-Person Being* (2004) and *The Knowing Animal: A Philosophical Inquiry into Knowledge and Truth* (2005). The trilogy's overall title is *Handkind*.

(and their brains) nor our agency, neither our animal sentience nor our human knowledge; that gives due credit to our brains and at the same time acknowledges just how far we have transcended them.

NOTE ON PUBLISHING HISTORY

A Pocket Lexicon of Neuromythology has had a checkered publishing history. It was planned as part of a book, *The Explicit Animal: A Defence of Human Consciousness*, which was published by Macmillan over a decade ago, but proved difficult to accommodate. It was therefore issued separately, by a small publisher, the Ferrington Press, under the whimsical title *Psycho-Electronics or A Guide in the Form of a Lexicon to the Pseudo-Science of Cognitive Mechanics*. Ferrington then ran into difficulties and the book disappeared without leaving much of a trace behind it. It was distributed largely by the author, as a free gift to anyone who showed an interest. In 1999, I included it, under its present title, in a book of essays, also published by Macmillan, *On the Edge of Certainty*. The only attention it has attracted in the decade or so since its publication was a very sympathetic review in the *Journal of Consciousness Studies*. I am therefore enormously grateful to Anthony Freeman, managing editor of *JCS* and its publishing company Imprint Academic, not only for publicising this little book the first time round, but also for giving it this third chance. Perhaps this time the points it tried to make will be taken on board by the neuromythologists whose use of language is still largely unchallenged.

Raymond Tallis MA FRCP DLitt LittD FMed Sci

Manchester, 2004

PREFATORY NOTE (1994)

This pocket dictionary of neuromythology arose as a by-product
— but not, I hope, as a waste product — of the writing of another
book, *The Explicit Animal* (1991), a critique of contemporary
materialistic accounts of human consciousness. During the
course of writing that book, I became conscious that certain
terms were used repeatedly and that the use, or more precisely
misuse, of these terms lay at the heart not only of the errors in
neurobiological and computational theories of the mind but also
of their apparent explanatory force. It seemed to me that a critical dictionary of such terms would be as effective as a more conventional continuous argument as a way of refuting the dreams
and fantasies of the artificial intelligentsia and others who
would assimilate minds to brains and brains to machines.
Although *Psycho-Electronics* is complementary to *The Explicit
Animal* and may be read in conjunction with it, it does stand on
its own as the arguments given in the entries are complete.

A handful of texts — notably P.N. Johnson-Laird's *The Computer and the Mind* (1988) — has been drawn upon repeatedly as
the source of the views criticised here. This is in a sense unfair, as
they have been selected mainly because they provide the best
expressions of these views. In other words, they have been
singled out for their merits — of clarity in particular — rather
than for their deficiencies. My dissent from the ideas advanced
in these texts in no way diminishes my indebtedness to them.

I am enormously grateful to Mark Rogers who has enabled
this Lexicon to see the light of day and who read the manuscript
with great care and made many useful suggestions which have
been incorporated into the text.

INTRODUCTION (1994)

Thinking By Transferred Epithet

A *picture* held us captive. And we could not get outside of it for it lay in our language and language seemed to repeat it to us inexorably. (Wittgenstein, 1953, p. 115)

Both biological and computational models of consciousness depend for their apparent plausibility upon the use of certain terms that have a multiplicity of meanings. These terms are popular with theorists because within the shades of their voluminous connotative folds, arguments that would not stand up in broad daylight may seem to carry conviction. The reader or listener, in allowing the use of the terms, does not know what he is taking on. The most important characteristic of these terms is that they have a foot in both camps: they can be applied to machines as well as to human beings and their deployment erodes, or elides, or conjures away, the barriers between man and machine, between consciousness and mechanism. The usual sequence of events is that a term most usually applied to human beings is transferred to machines. This begins as a consciously metaphorical or specialist use but the special, restricted, basis for the anthropomorphic language is soon forgotten: the metaphorical clothes in which thinking is wrapped become its skin. Machines described in human terms are then offered as models for mind (described in slightly machine-like terms).

To see what is wrong with the vast majority of philosophical discourse in the field of cognitive science, and what is amiss with physicalist accounts of the mind generally, we need to look particularly carefully at the first step: the application of human terms to machines. In most cases, as we shall see, the process of epithet transfer is no more valid (or no less metaphorical) than referring to the place used to house candidates for execution as 'a condemned cell'. When we hear of a man who has spent the last year in a condemned cell, we know that it is the man, not the cell, who faces execution. It is the man, not the cell, who should have right of appeal. It is the man, not the cell, on whose behalf we grow indignant. When we are told that a telephone receives information, however, we fail to notice — or at least fail to be alerted by — the fact that it is we, not the telephone, who require, are able to receive, and are glad of, *information.[41] This is not because there is more justification in taking the transferred epithet literally in the case of the telephone than in the case of the prison cell but because '*information' has a multiplicity of meanings that 'condemn' does not. In the case of the telephone, the transferred epithet adopts a protective colouring to suit its new surroundings.

It is not too much of an exaggeration to claim that the greatest advances in breaking down the mind/body, consciousness/ mechanism, man/machine barriers have come not from neurobiology or computer science but from the use of transferred epithets. The engineer's customary courtesy in his dealings with his machines (not qualitatively different from that which prompts sailors to refer to their ships as 'she') has permitted many assertions to pass 'on the nod' that would otherwise be challenged. Indeed, such courtesies have come so to dominate our language that it is almost impossible to look critically at the idea that machines have *memories, that they 'store *information' and do *calculations, or that different parts of the nervous system 'signal' to one another. We are so accustomed to hearing that radar 'sees' an enemy plane or that it 'hunts' a target that we have ceased to notice how we are conferring intentionality upon systems that are themselves only prosthetic extensions of the conscious human body.

Epithet transfer is, I have indicated, two-way: machines are described anthropomorphically and, at the same time, the anthropic terms in which they are described undergo a machine-ward shift. These same terms, modified by their life amongst the machines, can then be re-applied to minds and the impression is then created that minds and machines are one. To cross the machine/mind barrier, it is not sufficient to make the mind machine-like; one must do so using terms that have already unobtrusively mentalised machines. If you make machines into

---

[41]   The presence of an asterisk * indicates a technical term discussed in this Lexicon; see the alphabetical listing below.

minds by describing them in mental terms, you are already half way to making minds into machines. The awaiting terminology is more friendly. As a result, it is possible to overlook, for example, that seeing a computer as anything other than an unconscious automaton is crude animism.

This journeying of terms between the mental and the physical realms lies at the root of the myth that modern neurological science has somehow explained, or will explain, or has advanced our understanding of, what consciousness truly is. My concern is thus with the foundations of *neuromythology*, a pseudo-science that exploits the justified prestige of neuroanatomy, neurophysiology, neurochemistry and the other legitimate neurosciences. The terms that I have selected for this critical dictionary of neuromythology seem to me the most important among those that are responsible for carrying discourse painlessly — indeed almost unwittingly — across the man/mechanism divide. They are vital to the illusion that machine models of consciousness — whether wet biological or dry computational — have explanatory force. Indeed Janus-faced words like '*memory' and '*information' — which look in the direction of both man and machines — seem to dissolve the very problems that philosophically are most interesting. In consequence, most neurologically-based biological and computational explanations of consciousness begin beyond the point where the real questions are to be found. The terminology starts, as it were, on the far side of the answers. If this dictionary serves any purpose at all, I hope that, by showing the hollowness of the answers built into the terminology, it will restore the questions and the sense of the mystery of human consciousness.

One final preliminary point. At the time that this Lexicon was conceived, I had not read Peter Hacker's 1987 contribution to *Mindwaves*. On reading Hacker, I discovered that I was not unique in my critical attitude towards the language of neuromythology. His excellent piece, which makes many of the points covered in this dictionary, is strongly recommended. It should be compulsory reading for anyone — neurobiologist, cognitive psychologist or philosopher — proposing to mix neurology and metaphysics.

The Lexicon

An orator uses ink to trace out his writing; does that mean that ink is a highly eloquent liquid? (Jean-Jacques Rousseau *Essai sur l'origine des langes*, 1970 ed., Paris, p. 149)

CALCULATIONS (COMPUTATIONS)

According to Johnson-Laird, the

> key concept [of cognitive science] is computation . . . Cognitive science tries to elucidate the workings of the mind by treating them as computations, not necessarily of the sort carried out by the familiar digital computer, but of a sort that lies within this broader framework of the theory of computation. (Johnson-Laird, 1988, p. 9)

This view is reiterated at the end of his book: 'Mental processes are the computations of the brain'(p. 391).

In its original (and still very much living) sense, computation is concerned solely with calculation. The Oxford English Dictionary defines 'computation' as:

> The action or process of computing, reckoning or counting; a method or system of reckoning; arithmetical or mathematical calculation.

Computation extends beyond calculation in the narrowly defined sense of 'doing sums'. Most definitions of computers include *logical as well as arithmetical operations, as do computational models of the mind.[1] Others extend the concept further

---

[1]   'Oversimplifying, one could think of the mind as essentially a kind of logic machine that operates on sentences' (Patricia Churchland, 1986, p. 252).

to include all aspects of '*information *processing'. For example, Paul Churchland asserts that the input states

> of organisms that display natural intelligence . . . *represent many more things than just numbers, and the 'computations' they execute are concerned with far more things than mere arithmetical relations. They are also concerned with *logical relations, for example, and with spatial shapes, social relations, linguistic structures, color, motion, and so forth. (Paul Churchland, 1988, p. 92)

Nevertheless, calculation in the ordinary sense remains the paradigm computation and the basis of all the other computations. The computer expresses its 'concern' with logical relations, spatial shapes etc. in sums of various sorts — vector transformations etc. For example, a computer builds up an image by assigning digital values to the elements of the image and manipulating the digits. So, in looking critically at computational models of the mind, it is legitimate to focus on calculations.

There are two relevant questions:

(1) Is the mind essentially a calculator?

(2) Do computers actually calculate?

(1) Is the mind essentially a calculator?

This is a rather complex question, taking in many subsidiary questions; for example: can the mind be made up of calculations? does a whole lot of calculations add up to a mind? do they somehow throw in their lot together to make something bigger than themselves? can computational calculations amount to a mind that can, among other things, consciously calculate?

Suppose we took seriously the idea that the mind is like a mass of calculations or, in some non-trivial sense, analogous to it, we would have to identify what it is about the calculations themselves (as opposed to *someone doing the calculations*) that is mind-like. What is quasi-conscious about 2+2=4? (I have taken a short calculation because there is no reason why a long calculation should be more like a mind than a short one. Or a calculation with many steps spread over a period of time be closer to mind at any given moment than a one-step calculation). What is it about

2+2=4 that makes it closer to mind than 2 alone? In what, according to this model, does the mind reside? The individual symbols? The plus sign between them? The result, i.e. 4? If mind is a
matter of computation, on which side of the equation is it to be
found? Does mind reside in *moving towards* a result? Or is mind
the result itself — or a heap of results? And what of my awareness of doing a sum — as when I *consciously* calculate the square
root of 81 — is this a meta-sum, a sum of sums, or a sum that
manages, mysteriously, to be about itself?

It is enough to pose the questions in this way, to take the computational model with sufficient literalness to denude it of a
nimbus of vagueness, to discredit it. It is obvious that the mind,
or 'mind-ness', cannot reside in any of the things considered in
the preceding paragraph; or not, at least, in any one of them
more than any of the others. Nor in all of them together — for in
what (or how) would they come together? Nor is there any reason for believing that the mind resides in the operation of
sentential (as opposed to numerical) calculus, as Patricia
Churchland suggests (p. 37 above, note 1) or any other kinds of
mathematical or logical operations, such as vector-to-vector
transformation, as suggested by Paul Churchland (p. 38 above).
The same unanswerable questions arise irrespective of whether
the operations are performed on numbers, sentences or abstract
entities such as vectors. Patricia Churchland's suggestion that
mind 'is a kind of *logic machine* operating on sentences' (italics
mine) advances the even more implausible notion of mind
as being located not in the *operations* of the computer (or the
Arithmetic-Logic Unit) but being identified with the machine
itself — either the material of which it is made or the electronic
'structure' that can be abstracted from it.

So it is difficult to see how one could make sense of — never
mind prove or test — the idea that the mind is number- (or logic-)
crunching. To suggest that it is seems anyway to invert the hierarchy of levels of conscious activity. Common sense suggests
that sensations are more primitive than abstract ideas and that
abstract ideas are more primitive than the numerical or logical
operations performed upon them. The notion that the basic
material of mind is logico-numeric runs counter to this intuitive

ordering. Since, moreover, logico-numeric operations must pre-suppose sensations if the mind is to get a purchase on the world, computational theories of the mind seem to be like an Escher staircase where the top flight (the most sophisticated function of mind) is found to underlie the bottom flight (sensation). Granted, science progresses by criticising and overthrowing our intuitions, by undermining common sense, but it has to adduce powerful reasons for this. The evidence that this inverted hierar-chy has little basis — and that mind is therefore not computer-like — comes from the observation that, whereas for computers enormously complex calculations are 'elementary' and achiev-ing the equivalent of ordinary perception beyond their reach, for minds the opposite holds.

(2) Do computers actually calculate in the sense necessary to support the computational theory of mind?

The assumption that computers calculate seems so self-evident it is hardly visible. Nevertheless, it is legitimate to ask whether they really can do this — in the sense that you and I calculate; whether pocket calculators calculate — in the sense that those who use them calculate; whether brains calculate — in the sense that people do. The (to some surprising) answer to all these ques-tions is: No. Calculating machines are extensions of the mind, yes; but they are are mind-like (or perform mental functions) only in conjunction with minds. They are mental prostheses or orthoses, not stand-alone minds. In the absence of a conscious-ness derived from somewhere else, the electrical events occur-ring in computers are just that — and not calculations.

Surely it makes sense to speak of a computer performing a cal-culation? Yes; but only in the limited way in which it makes sense to say that watches tell the time. Watches tell the time only if they are consulted by someone to whom the symbols on the face make sense. More generally, they require an interpreting consciousness to whom to tell the time. The *meaning* of the events in the watch — as a continuous statement of what time it is — is not intrinsic to them. And if, for example, there were a nuclear catastrophe that wiped out all conscious life on the planet, the watch face, arrested at the moment of the explosion, would not constitute a standing assertion to the effect that 'It is five past eight' or 'The explosion took place at five past eight'. Of course one can imagine a subsequent time, thousands of years after the explosion, when the descendents of those survivors who happened to be away from the planet when it took place, visit Earth and come across the watch. To them, the watch would seem to be stating the time of the explosion. They might be tempted to think of the watch as having *stored *information* about the time of the explosion. But this would only be as legitimate or illegitimate as the claim that the scorched rocks and other evidences of devastation stored *information about the catastrophe.

The calculating computer is precisely analogous to the time-telling watch. I can calculate to, and for, myself. A computer can 'calculate' only for others and those others have to be conscious. The events that take place in a computer do not count as calculations without the presence of an interpreting consciousness to transform the electrical events into meaningful symbols. Consciousness, unlike a calculator or a watch, makes sense to/of/for itself.

Now it might be argued that 'more *complex' computers do, indeed, calculate. Consider, for example, a robot that, on the basis of the distribution of light energy reaching certain photo-sensitive plates, is able to avoid bumping into an obstacle. It could be argued that it, or its computer, had indeed calculated in order to determine its position in relation to the obstacle and had acted upon the result of that calculation. In other words, that it must have carried out a calculation since it could not otherwise have consumed or used the result of the calculation. The force of this argument comes from the fact that, in contrast to the case of the watch 'telling the time', the computer seems to be doing something with the events occurring within it; it seems to be using the result, just as a conscious being would use it.

The fault of this argument is that it anthropomorphises the output of the computer/robot. The robot is not really acting, in the sense of consciously achieving a certain end. So it is not using the result of the calculation in the way that conscious humans use calculations. And so it is not really calculating in the true

sense of the term. A calculation is an act; the events in the computer are no more acts than its inputs are acts. The algorithm that
relates the input to the output isn't also able to transform an
input of events into an output of acts.

Even the most *sophisticated computer is no more capable of
'calculating', in the way that you or I do, than is a five pound calculator bought at a garage. One could labour this point by saying
that calculators, irrespective of their power, calculate without
feeling the qualitative size of the quantities they 'handle'. Moreover, the events that take place in the logic circuits of the cheap
calculator — which I presume few people would claim to be conscious — are essentially the same as occur, on a much larger
scale, in, say, a Super-Cray. In which case, the fact that computers calculate (in this sense) does nothing to carry them over the
mind–machine barrier. Attributing calculating power or calculating activity to evidently unconscious machines does the computational theory of consciousness no service whatsoever. For it
disassociates computation from consciousness.

Curiously, that there is nothing intrinsically *conscious* about
computing or even computational events in the brain is often
emphasised by the most ardent computational theorists of consciousness. What, then, are we to make of the explanatory status
of the claim that 'mental processes are the computations of the
brain' if all sides agree that the vast majority of 'cerebral computations' are unconscious? *The truth is, we cannot hold that the brain
is a computational machine* and *that it carries out calculations, most of
which are unconscious* and *that these calculations are the basis of (and
the essence of) consciousness.* If the unconscious calculations of the
cerebellum ('a neuronal machine') — which permit navigation
through the world by automatic pilot dead reckoning — are the
paradigm of the computational activity of the brain, then such
activity must have little to offer by way of explanation of consciousness, and its typical manifestations — such as deliberately
picking one's way across the world, and knowing why one is
doing it, and where and who one is.

To summarise, machines do not of themselves calculate. If the
brain is a machine it cannot really compute or perform calculations without a consciousness external to it to transform the

events that take place in it into 'computational activity'. Those events cannot themselves therefore constitute consciousness or mental processes. This is in fact half-acknowledged by computational theorists who recognise that the vast majority of the 'calculations' that take place even in the simultaneously anthropomorphised and physicalised cerebral machines are unconscious: they neither enter, nor contribute to the making of, consciousness.

There is some interesting equivocation by Johnson-Laird on the question of the computational model of the mind. Is the mind a computational phenomenon? he asks. No one knows, he replies. But then adds:

> *Theories* of the mind, however, should not be confused with the mind itself, any more than theories of the weather should be confused with rain or sunshine. And what is clear is that computability provides an appropriate conceptual apparatus for theories of the mind. (Johnson-Laird, 1988, p. 51)

He then asserts that 'this apparatus takes nothing for granted that is not obvious — any computation can always be reduced, if need be, to a finite set of instructions for shifting a tape and writing binary code on it'. It is, of course, not at all clear that computability provides 'an appropriate conceptual apparatus for theories of the mind'. This may be why Johnson-Laird, a few lines later, adopts the baldly prescriptive position that 'theories of mind should be expressed in a form that can be modelled on a computer program'. This prescription may make the theories testable (in a way that will satisfy cognitive psychologists) but will not ensure that they are not misconceived. We have here an example of how methodological constraints on the investigation of something start to dictate the way we see that thing. Johnson-Laird's position seems to be that there is little or no evidence either way as to whether or not the mind is a computational phenomenon but we may as well assume that it is because it produces interesting and testable (i.e. computer modellable) theories. One is reminded of the drunk who having lost his key in a dark street looks for it next to the street lamp, not because he thinks the key is there, but because that is where the light is.

COMPLEXITY (SOPHISTICATION)

> There are *materialist* theories of mind, theories which claim that
> what we call mental states and processes are merely sophisti-
> cated states and processes of a complex system. (Paul
> Churchland, 1988, p. 2)

Talk about 'sophisticated' machines (or 'sophisticated' states of
such machines) is so commonplace — both in everyday parlance
and in the discourses of cognitive scientists and other machine
theorists of the mind — that it is difficult to remember that it
represents an extremely gross case of epithet transfer. The
epithet transfer is from the minds of the people who dreamt up
and created the machine to the machine itself; or from the
description of the functions or purposes that it serves to the sup-
posedly inherent properties of the machine. Of course, in most
cases, talk about the 'sophistication' of machines is not intended
literally. It is meant rather loosely, as when we speak of a 'clever
design', where the (conscious) cleverness is, of course, a property of the designer rather of the object he has designed (cf.
'smart' cards). Sometimes, however, it *is* meant literally, as when
philosophers and other theorists adduce 'the increasing sophistication' of computers as indicating that they will more closely
approximate consciousness. ('As computers become increasingly sophisticated, so they will become more mind-like.') In
either case, it is as if it is expected that a bit of the sophistication
of the minds of the engineers will rub off on the machines and
awaken them from their mechanistic slumbers.

Even more widely used than 'sophisticated' (which should,
after all, be rather too obviously anthropomorphic a term to be
taken seriously) is 'complex' (and 'complexity'). 'Complex', too,
is an anthropomorphism or a transferred epithet when applied
to machines or unconscious matter but it is more difficult to spot
this. It is important to do so because the term carries enormous
spurious explanatory force.

It is often stated that new properties can emerge in complex
machines that are not evident either in simpler machines or in
the components of more complex machines. Complexity is
appealed to as that which will explain the emergence of 'higher'
functions. At a certain '*level' of complexity, consciousness will

emerge or 'supervene'. The brain, for example, is 'incredibly complex' and this fact should disarm our surprise that it uniquely carries consciousness.

By what criteria does the brain count as complex? The most obvious is that we do not understand it and, indeed, have very great difficulty in making progress towards understanding it. But that criterion is clearly not good enough for a thoroughgoing physicalism, as it is too obviously subjective and anthropomorphic. Besides it does not generate the discriminations we need. After all, there is nothing in the world that we understand fully, and the harder we try to understand something, the harder it becomes to understand. Modern physics has revealed how infinitely complex common or garden matter is.

So more 'objective' markers of complexity are invoked. The brain, we are to understand, is sufficiently complex to support higher functions because it is composed of some 10,000,000,000 neurons; and, as if this were not sufficient to leave one gape-mouthed with uncritical awe, it is pointed out that each of these components connects with numerous other components, so that the possible number of sub-units or combinations exceeds the number of atoms in the universe. With that kind of kit on board, *anything* must be possible.

Unfortunately, this does not amount to an objective case for the special complexity of the brain. For any object can be seen to be composed of a very large number of units. Just *how* large will depend upon how it is looked at. A pebble, for example, may be seen as one large lump or as many billions of atom-sized pieces. And the same applies to combinations of its components. We may abstract an infinite number of different sub-sets of atoms from a pebble. The argument that these subsets do not have any real existence because they do not work together in a co-ordinated way, unlike the subsystems we can identify in the brain, does not wash either, because all atoms in some sense can be regarded as influencing all other atoms and one could generate an enormously (indeed, 'incredibly') complex description that would summarise the combined influence of one sub-set of atoms upon another.

If the pebble example does not convince, one could point to huge, explicitly organised interacting systems in plants and nonconscious animals in which the supposed emergent properties of consciousness have not emerged. But to do so would be to miss the point which is this: *'complexity' is not an intrinsic feature of certain states and arrangements of matter*. No one bit of matter has a right to be thought of as intrinsically more complex than any other. Complexity is in the eye of the beholder and it reflects our ability, or more precisely our inability, to comprehend the object in question. In relation to human artifacts, our measures of complexity will reflect our estimate of the ingenuity and multiplicity of the thoughts and processes that led to its manufacture. When we speak of complex systems, we are as surely transferring epithets from minds to machines as we are when we speak of sophistication. To suggest that complexity leads to mind is to put the cart before the horse; for it is mind that finds, and defines, complexity.

Compare, here, the concept of 'order'. Writers often speak of 'highly ordered systems'. Is this an objective property of certain bits of matter compared with some others? Apparently not; the harder one looks at any bit of matter, the more one will find order and disorder, according to the criteria one chooses. For there is no objective measure of order. Nor is there of 'degree of complexity of orderedness'. A system may be ordered or disordered, depending on how it is described. One could go further: a piece of matter may be a system or not, depending on how it is described. Strictly, physicalism knows no systems (or systems as opposed to non-systems).

FODOR

Not a term used by cognitive scientists but a philosopher of cognitive science whose work lies at the very heart of most of the muddles dealt with in this Lexicon — which could as well be entitled 'A Critical Dictionary of Fodorese'. A separate *ad hominem* critique would be excessively tedious. However, connoisseurs of homuncularity, anthropomorphosophistry and transferred epithets might like to savour the following sentence from an article on Vygotsky:

> It is tempting (perhaps it is mandatory) to explain such interactions [between the senses] by assuming that sensory channels transduce stimulus data into a central *computing *language rich enough to *represent visual, tactile, auditory, gustatory and olfactory *information as well as whatever abstract conceptual apparatus is involved in thought. (Fodor, 1972)

GOALS
(FUNCTIONS, OBJECTS, PURPOSES, AIMS, PLANS)

Human beings have goals. Their actions, and the things that assist them in their actions, have functions, purposes, objects, aims. They formulate plans in order to execute actions and achieve their objects and purposes. And so on. All of this seems sufficiently obvious, though twenty or thirty years ago the realisation that behaviour was not controlled and shaped entirely by external events but by plans, aims and goals counted as one of the great discoveries (or re-discoveries) of psychology. Prior to that time, behaviourist dogma had forbidden acknowledgement of the obvious. Since then, the wheel has come full circle: once nobody had goals; now everything has; once it was heresy to attribute sense of purpose to human beings; now it is quite acceptable to attribute it to lower organisms and even machines. Even automata have feelings, it seems.

'When you develop a plan', Johnson-Laird says, in his excellent exposition of Newell and Simon's study of plans, 'you have in mind an *initial state* and a *goal,* and your task is to devise a sequence of *operations* [a production system] that will get you from one to the other.'[2] Well, possibly, though this description sounds as if it suffers a little from the widespread complaint of *misplaced explicitness.* This is not surprising because it conflates the normal execution of a plan with the process of getting a machine to execute one of our plans or of devising a machine that will do this. That is not too worrying. What is worrying is that the subsequent discussion of plans and productions moves seamlessly between machines, machine designers and human

[2]   Johnson-Laird, 1988, pp. 159 et seq.

beings (in particular, children). Humans as well as machines seemingly execute sub-routines; machines as well as humans have sub-goals. A single description — production systems — encompasses both human beings engaged in purposeful, goal-orientated activity and the machines that human beings may use to assist such activities.

It should be unnecessary to have to point out that (unconscious) automata do not have goals; and if they execute plans, it is our plans (of which they are quite unaware) that they execute, not their own. But it is all too easy to slip from a valid teleological account of a machine (or a process within an organism, or a sub-system within the brain) to an anthropomorphised account of it; to move from saying 'the aim of this machine is to . . .' to 'this machine aims to . . .'. Why we tend to make these attributions is explained by Searle in his classic paper:

> it has to do with the fact that in artifacts we extend our own intentionality; our tools are extensions of our purposes, and so we find it natural to make metaphorical attributions of intentionality to them. (Searle, 1980; cf. Searle 1987)

And so we drift by stages to the absurd position, such as that adopted by John McCarthy (which Searle's scorn has made famous), in which even simple devices such as thermostats perceive things and try to change them. McCarthy's suggestions are crass but at least they do not try to clothe their crassness in smoke-screen talk about *complexity. Moreover, they have been defended, by, for example, Dennett.

Dennett has advanced a curious defence of the attribution of intentionality to machines.[3] 'The intentional stance', according to Dennett, has enormous predictive advantage and can be understood and justified solely in terms of these advantages (rather than on the basis of the objective reality of intentionality). If we were to try to predict the next move of a chess playing machine, for example, we would not have a hope of doing so unless we appreciated its purpose. More specifically, our best strategy is to assume that it has a *goal,* that it is *trying to win the game.* Only this would make sense of its activities or, to describe

---

[3]   Dennett (1971).

this less contentiously, of the events observed to take place in it; only thus would we come anywhere near to predicting (and understanding) its output. The intentional stance — which is neither the physical stance (no-one could hope to predict the output of a chess machine from considering its molecular structure) nor the design stance (for the design of chess-playing machines is so complex that designers may not predict how the machine will respond to a particular move) — justifies one in thinking of the machine as having certain Information available to it, as possessing certain goals and, on the basis of these, working out the best move. According to Dennett, it is then 'a small step to calling the information possessed by computers beliefs, its goals and subgoals its *desires*'.

The same considerations, Dennett believes, apply to animal organisms — and to human beings. I could, in theory, predict your behaviour from a consideration of your molecular structure and content and applying the laws of physics — the Laplacean approach. But this would be extremely laborious and require an almost infinite amount of knowledge. A much quicker way will be to assume the intentional stance and work out what you are going to do next on the basis that you believe certain things and desire to bring about certain ends.

Dennett's defence of the attribution of goals and other intentional states to machines is perverse. It implies that there is as much justification in crediting machines with such states as in crediting humans with them because in all cases doing so is merely an expedient to aid prediction. The intentional stance *in all cases* is just a 'manner of speaking' or, more precisely, a manner of describing: 'goals', 'beliefs', 'desires' etc. are not peculiar entities but essential components of the most effective *description* of the systems (machines, animals, humans) in question. Dennett, in other words, *is able to defend the ascription of intentionality to machines by denying the objective reality of intentionality*. Machines have goals in the sense that humans have; and humans do not 'really' have goals, just as machines don't. The intentional stance is as much 'as if' for humans as for machines. Goals are ascribed — to 'intentional systems', that is to say to systems considered for the purposes of effective description as intentional — but they are not possessed by, inherent in, etc. the systems or entitities themselves. This is a peculiar twist to the transfer of epithet story: the goals and other intentional states we ascribe to humans have themselves been transferred from the descriptions that, only for purposes of predictive power, attribute them to many *complex systems. Intentionality isn't in the system but in the eye of the beholder of the system; in the tongue and pen of the describer of the system!

Dennett's position is a curious one. According to him, *my goal in trying to explain his ideas exists only as an attribution to me (this human system)*. In the absence of an interpreter of my behaviour I would be goal-less. This is in itself absurd but it is also incomprehensible. For it does not account for the power, the usefulness, of intentional explanations (if they are just *a façon de parler);* nor, more importantly, does it deal with the apparent intentionality of the descriptions themselves. In adopting the intentional stance towards a machine or a human being, I am surely in an intentional state. My descriptions are, after all, *about* their objects. Intentionality is therefore real. The democratising move of asserting that ascribing intentionality to machines is as justified (or unjustified) as ascribing it to humans misfires.

One final point. What does it *mean* to attribute goals, objects, purposes etc. to machines? Or to programmes (McCarthy attributes intentions to programmes)? Does a chess playing programme really *hope* to come out on top or at least to break even? Does it *want* to win? Does it *try?* Does it feel satisfied if it wins? Does it feel disppointed, frustrated, ashamed if it doesn't? Or are satisfaction, frustration etc. secondary things that are not part of goal-pursuit? The answers to these questions do not, I think, need spelling out.

GRAMMAR

Grammar is a very handy word for mediating between minds, brains and computers. Cognitive scientists and others will readily talk of the grammar of the brain, of the grammars of computer programmes and of the grammar inherent in the natural languages used by conscious speakers. Grammar here is clearly something rather larger and more exotic than that grammar we learned (and mis-spelled) in school.

During the period in which cognitive science has been establishing itself, the term grammar as used by linguists has undergone spectacular transformations. In the olden days, grammar had rather a narrow group of senses. It was first of all a branch of the study of a language that dealt with 'its inflexional forms or other means of indicating the relations of words in the sentence, and the *rules for employing these in accordance with established usage' (OED). It was concerned with seemingly superficial features of language; with visible syntax, inflexion and word-formation. Grammar tended at times to be prescriptive, evaluating and correcting speech and writing that did not conform to accepted usage. The relation between grammar and the consciousness of the speaker was quite an intimate one: speakers were, to a lesser or greater extent, aware of speaking grammatically. The *rules of grammar could be taught and were anyway available in books — 'grammars'.

With the advent of scientific (and sometimes scientistic) linguistics, this has changed. Grammar is now understood more widely as that part of the systematic description of language which accounts for the way in which words are combined to form sentences. Syntactic theory is an attempt to describe the general principles of sentence construction that speakers must know implicitly in order to use sounds to convey meanings. At its most ambitious, a grammar of a language is a theory or set of statements that tell us in an explicit way which combinations of the basic elements of the language are permitted and which are not: it may be seen as a device for generating all the well-formed formulae of the language and no ill-formed ones. It is an exploration of the *system* of language, of the *rules in accordance with which an infinite number of sentences can be generated out of combinations of a finite number of words. Grammarians conceive of a total grammar which will encompass all the *rules necessary to generate the entire corpus of well-formed sentences in a language and to exclude the inadmissible ones. Hence Chomsky's generative syntax that dreams of becoming a complete account of the *rules according to which the rule-governed creativity of the natural language speaker operates. Grammars know themselves for the first time: they are sets of rules for domains of symbols (or languages) that characterise all the properly formed constructions, and provide a description of their structure.

Since Saussure, linguists and others have become accustomed to the idea that the greater part of the system is actually hidden from the language user. There has been a decreasing emphasis upon the *rules the individual knows and has been taught by other individuals — so-called surface features of syntax — and more upon those *rules which can be discerned in language by experts, though they are unknown to the ordinary speakers who nevertheless conform to them.

Modern grammar, then, is concerned with the form of language rather than its accidents and with deep structures available to objective observation and analysis rather than surface features and *rules available directly to subjective intuitions. It connects naturally with the idea of language as a system that drives itself, rather than being driven by users; an autonomous structure that requisitions voices for its realisation; a structuralist *langue* that speaks through speakers rather than being spoken by them.

The *rules prove to be so complex and so numerous that it seems unlikely that they can be learned, never mind taught. Parents do not teach children their native languages; they simply provide an environment in which they can be acquired. The acquisition of language is the work not of a conscious individual or of the product of interactions between conscious individuals. The speed of acquisition of the *rules, and on the basis of such poor quality material, argues for a special faculty in the brain for extracting grammars from rather unstructured presentations. This faculty, the Language Acquisition Device, is primed with a Universal Grammar which it can then apply to the particular linguistic material served up to it.

With Chomsky, then, the concept of grammar was consequently separated decisively from grammar books, from the conscious application of *rules of good discourse, and from correctable lapses. It went underground, hidden in the deep structures discerned by experts and buried in the notional organ of the brain that did the work of the language learner for him. This created a favourable background for its use as one of the key metaphors in the development of cognitive science and for the invasion of brains by grammars, codes and languages.

One of the first beneficiaries of structural and subsequently Chomskeian approaches to language was computerese. A grammar was 'a device' connecting an input to an output, operating on the raw material of individual symbols to produce the finished product of sentences. A grammar could be seen as a set of algorithms. It was but a short step to see a general relation between programmes and grammars. The output of any programme can be captured in a grammar. But a grammar by itself can do nothing. It is waiting to be used to produce symbols or analyse them. Programmes, however, are capable of doing things. They can use a grammar to produce or process strings of symbols.

A grammar is a kind of machine (and language was described in machine terms by Chomsky and everyone who followed him). And machines — in particular computers — have grammars: there is a grammar of their behaviour. Other things have grammars: there is a grammar of the behaviour, or, indeed, of all the input–output relations, of organisms.

A word that passes so readily between brains, organisms and computers has obviously considerable attractions for someone wanting to cross the machine–brain barrier. But what of the mind–brain barrier. How can it ease the passage across this impermeable wall? For some this presents no problem. Consciousness, or the mind, is cast in language — 'the language of thought' or 'mentalese'. This — despite its title — need not be a language used or participated in consciously. The massive unconscious depths Chomsky and structuralists have uncovered in language in the form of the grammar and deep structures permits the language of thought to be something that is not necessarily accessible to the thinker nor corresponding to what we would normally recognise as a language. However, such a language lies at the root of thoughts and languages as we more usually understand them. It is from the language of thought that natural languages derive their peculiar properties.

> The basic concept is simple but striking. Assume that there are such things as mental symbols (mental representations) and that mental symbols have semantic properties ... The semantic properties of the words and sentences we utter are in turn inherited from the semantic properties of the mental states that language expresses. (Fodor, 1981)

There is, *Fodor also tells us, 'a considerable consensus ... that there is a "semantic" level of grammatical *representation — a level at which the meaning of sentences is formally specified.'[4] The language of thought is 'the medium for computations underlying cognitive *processes'.[5]

Grammar has an additional attractive ambiguity: like that of 'history', which may be used to mean either what happened in the past or the study of what happened in the past, i.e. historiography. This ambiguity — which allows grammar to be both something someone is conscious of and the *rules according to which someone acts irrespective of whether he is conscious of them — makes it a very useful passport across the brain–mind barrier.

INFORMATION (KNOWLEDGE)

This is the big one, an absolutely key term in cognitive science and much contemporary thought about brain function, the mind and the relationship between them. According to popular thought, what, above all, the mind–brain does is acquire, *process and store information.

What is information? 'Information' is a term that has a multiplicity of senses, some everyday, some highly specialised and technical. Much of the explanatory force of 'informational' explanations of consciousness and the mind–brain depends upon unobserved shuttling back and forth between these various senses.

---

[4]　Fodor (1976), p. 125.
[5]　Fodor (1976), p. 65.

Let us begin at the beginning. The Oxford English Dictionary lists numerous senses of the word 'information'. The most important of these is: 'Knowledge communicated concerning some particular fact, subject or event; that of which one is apprised or told; intelligence, news'. This ordinary sense is very different from the specialised sense used widely in cognitive and other sciences.

At first the specialised, technical sense of information was to be kept quite separate from the ordinary sense, as was emphasised by the communication engineers who first intro-duced it. This specialised sense was occasioned by the need to *quantify* information, in order to evaluate the work done by, and the efficiency of, communication channels charged with trans-mitting it. It is worth looking at this in some detail because it has pervaded the entire universe of discourse of cognitive science.

Since to be informed is to learn something one did not know before, information can be understood as something that resolves an *uncertainty* about how things are or how they are going to be. Uncertainty itself can be quantified in relation to the number of possible states of affairs that might be the case. *In engineering terms,* the information content of a message is propor-tional to the amount of prior uncertainty it resolves. If there are only two possibilities, and hence only two possible messages, then the successful transmission of one of the messages — the actual message — will convey a selective information content of one bit or binary digit. The amount of information carried by any message will be determined by the number of possible alterna-tives that have been selected from and the relative prior proba-bilities of the different messages. The more unexpected, or unexpectable a message is, the greater its information content. A totally expected message, one that resolves no prior uncertain-ties, is redundant and, in engineering terms, has no information content: it is not worth paying for. Redundancy is both good and bad. It is good, inasmuch as it allows for a degradation of the message without loss of information transmission: the redun-dancy in written messages permits accurate decipherment of the most appalling handwriting, despite our inability to read certain individual letters. Redundancy is bad insofar as it may be uneconomical.

It will be clear from this that the engineer's sense of information, and in particular information content, has little to do with information in the ordinary sense. Weaver, one of the first to think of information in the way just described, underlined this:

> Information in this theory is used in a special sense that must not be confused with its ordinary usage. In particular, *information* must not be confused with meaning. In fact, two messages, one of which is heavily loaded with meaning, and the other of which is pure nonsense, can be exactly equivalent from the present viewpoint as regards information.[6]

Indeed the meaningful statement may have less information content than the meaningless one. Supposing A asks B if she loves him. B's 'Yes' is one of only two possible alternatives and, assuming he has no prior idea of the answer, will have an information content of one bit. Consider, by contrast, a meaningless message composed of randomly generated letters of the alphabet. At any given moment, if all letters are equally probable, then the occurrence of any one letter will have a likelihood of 1 in 26. This will give the letter/message an information content of between 4 and 5 bits — several times higher than that of the answer to the question 'Do you love me?' It is all a matter of the range of alternatives from which the message has been selected and their prior probabilities. As Shannon, another pioneer of the mathematical theory of communication, wrote, 'the semantic aspects of communication are irrelevant to the engineering aspects'.

In the specialised technical sense, then, information is measured by the reduction of uncertainty; the number of possibilities and their prior probabilities becomes a way of measuring information. Before long, this objective way of measuring information (which is quite separate from how *informative* — never mind how interesting, important, exciting — it seems to the recipient of the information) becomes a definition of information itself, the method of measuring the thing defines it: information

---

[6]   This passage and the quotation from Shannon below are cited by Hacker (1987). They come from Shannon and Weaver's classic text, *The Mathematical Theory of Communication* (1949).

is uncertainty reduction. And this uncertainty may not even have to be experienced as such by the individual but only inhere in the quantity of objective possibilities presented to him.

The engineering notion of information entered the sciences of the mind via the psychology of perception. From the early 1950s onwards, sensory perception was interpreted as the acquisition of information and sensory pathways were seen as channels transmitting information from the outside world to the centre. These 'channels' had 'limited information handling capacity'; they could cope with only so much at a time. Using the notion of information in the engineering sense, it was possible to make certain predictions that proved to be true. For example, Hick[7] found that the reaction time of human subjects to a stimulus depended on its selective information content; it depended, that is to say, not upon its actual content but upon the number of alternatives that had to be selected from. This, in turn, determined how much information had to be *processed before the subject could react. (The stimuli in question, it is not irrelevant to point out, were extremely simple: letters, numbers and simple pictures.)

From this, it was but a short step to see *perception* as information *processing and to regard the function of the nervous system as that of transmitting information from one place to another. It is a strange and contradictory move because it both dehumanises perception and anthropomorphises the organs of perception. The perceiver is placed on all fours with a telephone receiver, while the sense organs are treated as if they were devices that had certain goals and aims and functions. Nevertheless, over the last twenty years, the rhetoric of information has dominated thought about mental, cerebral and neuronal function. The apparent success of this mode of thought depends upon an almost continuous unacknowledged vacillation between the engineering and the ordinary senses of information. The information-theoretic account of perception makes intuitive sense because we think of the bearer of the nervous system being informed in the ordinary sense by what is going on in his ner-

---

[7]   Hick (1952).

vous system as well as acquiring information in the narrow sense of selecting between alternative possible states. By narrowing the conception of consciousness or awareness to that of being in receipt of information and widening that of information way beyond the engineering sense that gives it scientific respectability, and not acknowledging (or noticing) either of these moves, it seems possible to give a scientific, information-theoretic account of consciousness and of the nervous system. We can speak without embarrassment of consciousness as being the outcome of the information-processing activity of the nervous system.

It is worth dwelling on the inappropriateness of reducing consciousness to information. It amounts to expanding information to encompass the whole of awareness. Under this interpretation, an ordinary conscious being is literally steeped in information; the perceptual field is a multi-modal sphere of information. It is slightly odd, to say the least, to think of me, as I sit here in this room, as sitting in a sphere of information co-terminous with my sensory field; and equally odd to think of all-encompassing being-here as reducible to streams of data. Being situated does not quite amount to being informed — otherwise simply to be conscious would be to be well-informed to the point of saturation.

Unfortunately, not everyone is able to see the absurdity of this consequence of extending the notion of information to include all of conscious experience. Even fewer seem to be able to see that the engineer's use of the term information cannot apply outside of its legitimate provenance — that of devices designed by human beings to help them communicate with other human beings. Although information-content understood in engineering terms is distinct from meaning, its sense depends ultimately upon the intention to convey meaning, or to resolve uncertainty through the transmission of meaningful events. If we remove this essential element of human intentionality, in particular its involvement in acts and instruments of conscious and deliberate communication, then 'information states' or 'information-bearing states' can be made to encompass pretty well everything that happens or exists. The information-theoretic account of *perception* not only tries to have its conception of information in the aseptic, semantics-free scientific sense and eat it in the ordinary sense (otherwise the events in the afferent pathways would not count as perceptions), it also stands at the top of a slippery slope at the bottom of which lies the lunacy of those who claim that the entire universe is a process of transmitting and receiving information.

The first step down the slope carries information beyond the body, and devices that are designed to serve the information needs of human beings, into the energy incident upon the body. If one really believes that consciousness arises out of the interaction between the nervous system and objects outside of it, that it is the transfer of energy from external objects to sense endings that accounts for perception, then one has a problem. How does the *energy* impinging on the nervous system become transformed into *consciousness?* For, although the nervous system seems quite good at transducing various forms of energy into its own dialect of energy (propagated electrochemical changes), it doesn't seem to do anything corresponding to *the transformation of energy into information.*

One 'explanation' is that, while the events in the periphery of the nervous system are indeed energy-to-energy transductions, those that take place centrally somehow add up to a *pattern and this adding up to a pattern is an energy-to-information transformation. Why this is a non-explanation will be discussed in the entry on PATTERNS; for the present, we may content ourselves with the observation that patterns cannot be the basis of the consciousness- and information-bearing capability of the brain since patterns exist only insofar as they are discerned by consciousness. How, then, shall we account for the 'fact' that, according to Patricia Churchland, 'nervous systems are information processing machines'?[8] Clearly you can't process something you haven't got: a stomach isn't a dinner-processing machine unless it gets a dinner from somewhere. If the impulses in the nervous system convey information rather than making it themselves (as we are conventionally told) where does the information come from?

[8]   Patricia Churchland (1986), p. 36.

According to some it is actually present in the energy that impinges on the nervous system! The job of the nervous system is simply to extract and transmit it. Johnson-Laird notes approvingly that 'J.J. Gibson emphasised that light reflected from surfaces and focussed on the retina contains a large amount of information' (Gossipy stuff, light).[9] Astonishingly, this has been 'demonstrated' by Longuet-Higgins' analysis of the projective geometry of images. There are, however, no entirely free gifts: 'no matter how much information is in the light falling on the retinae, there must be mental mechanisms for recovering the identities of things in a scene and those of their properties that vision makes explicit to consciousness.' Still, the information in the light is a flying start . . .

This must surely be the easiest solution to the physicalist's puzzle of how (to use his own terms) energy is transformed into information: the information is *in* the energy; it simply has to be 'extracted' from it. The older magic thinking — the animistic intuition of 'mind among things' — has been supplanted by an 'informationistic' one.

This not the end, only the beginning, of the story. For some writers, information amongst things does not have to be extracted by the nervous system: it is there for the taking. Or, rather, it is there whether it is taken or not, irrespective of whether the information bearer interacts with the nervous system. According to some authors, not only are unconscious organisms information-processing devices, but the individual parts of them are as well. Indeed, information is embodied in all organisms, most notably in the genetic material. For example Richard Dawkins (whose views on this matter are by no means heterodox), takes it for granted that DNA is itself information, and carries instructions for transmitting and preserving information. 'If you want to understand life, don't think about vibrant throbbing gels and oozes, think about information technology.'[10] 'The information technology of the genes is digital . . . since we receive our inheritance in discrete particles.' The differ-

---

[9]   Johnson-Laird (1988), p. 14.
[10]   This and the following quotes are from Dawkins (1988).

ence between DNA and a floppy disc is merely a question of the storage medium used — chemical as opposed to electronic — but the essentials are the same. 'Each individual organism should be seen as a temporary vehicle in which DNA messages spend a tiny fraction of their geological lifetimes.' (pp. 126–7) And what an enormous number of messages there are! DNA is ROM (Read Only Memory) and it is comparable to a laser disc in terms of the amount of information it packs into a small space (pp. 152–3): 'at the molecular genetic level, every one of more than a trillion cells in the body contains about a thousand times as much precisely-coded digital information as my [Dawkins'] computer.' (p. xiii)

Such anthropomorphism — which makes the cells of my body infinitely better informed than I could ever hope to be — is not unusual and, indeed, has a long intellectual pedigree. It is rooted in a cluster of notions about the relations between *information, entropy and order.* Entropy is the degree of disorder in a system. Living systems, which are (according to the conceptual schema of one particular species of living system, namely man) uniquely ordered, therefore entrain a high degree of negative entropy. They are also highly improbable because of the universal tendency, expressed in the Second Law of Thermodynamics, for the degree of disorder in any system to increase. They should not come into being in the first place and should decay as soon as they do.

The argument behind the supposed relationship between information, entropy and order is well summarised by Colin Cherry:

> Entropy, in statistical thermodynamics, is a function of the probabilities of the states of the particles comprising a gas; information rate, in statistical communication theory, is a similar function of the probabilities of the states of a source. In both cases we have an *ensemble* — in the case of the gas, an enormous collection of particles, the states of which (i.e. the energies) are distributed according to some probability function; in the communication problem, a collection of messages, or states of a source, again described by a probability function. (Cherry, 1966, p. 215)

The idea that *information is equivalent to negative entropy* derives from Szilard's discussion of the Maxwell demon problem. The demon is conceived as receiving information about the particle motions of a gas on the basis of which he is able to direct particles to one side or another of a partition. As a result of this, the gas may be put in a highly ordered, lower entropy state. By this means, the information received by the demon enables him to increase the available energy in the system and the latter could drive a heat engine. Since doing so costs only 'information', the demon seems to have discovered the secret of a perpetual motion machine. The demon, in making use of his information in this way, is seemingly violating the Second Law. This is not, however, the case: he is not merely an observer of the system, he is also a participant; he is part of the system because he must receive energy in order to make his observations; he must be affected by the system in order to observe it. Szilard demonstrated that the selective action represented by the demon's observations results in an increase in entropy at least equal to the reduction in entropy he can effect by virtue of this information. There seems to be a trade off between entropy and information; from which it is concluded that information is, in a sense, negative entropy.

This analogy has a certain amount of intuitive attraction, as Cherry, from whose account of Szilard's thought experiment the above paragraph has been derived, explains:

> In a descriptive sense, entropy is often referred to as a 'measure of disorder' and the Second Law of Thermodynamics as stating that 'systems can only proceed to a state of increased disorder'; as time passes, 'entropy can never decrease'. The properties of a gas can change only in such a way that our knowledge of the positions and energies of the particles lessens; randomness always increases. In a similar descriptive way, information is contrasted, as bringing order out of chaos. Information is then said to be 'like' negative energy.

Cherry, however, warns against too literal an interpretation of these analogies and, even more severely, against too wide an application. Entropy is 'essentially a mathematical concept and the rules of its application are clearly laid down' and 'any likeness that exists [between negative entropy and information] exists between the mathematical descriptions which have been set up.' Moreover, the term entropy is usually applied to closed systems, which are utterly isolated and unable to exchange energy with their surroundings; while the latter are in a state of near-randomness and are enormous. This hardly applies to the communication systems in which humans and other organisms participate. Cherry's final comments on this matter are especially worth quoting:

> Mother Nature does not communicate to us with signs or language. A *communication channel* should be distinguished from a *channel of observation* and, without wishing to be too assertive, the writer would suggest that in true communication problems the concept of entropy need not be evoked at all. And again, physical entropy is capable of a number of interpretations, albeit related, and its similarity with (selective, syntactic) information is not as straightforward as the simplicity and apparent similarity of the formulae suggests. (p. 217)

Such warnings have gone unheeded by psychologists, for whom the sensory pathways as a channel of communication (and indeed the entire nervous system as an information transmission device) is an apparently undislodgeable received idea; by biologists; and by philosophers for whom the equation between order and information and information and mental function is beyond dispute.

The idea that order is information (and the preservation of order is the transmission of information through time — or *memory) is implicit in Dawkin's description of DNA as ROM. The equation between organic order and higher mental function is explicit in Paul Churchland's use of the entropy/information metaphors. Churchland at times seems to espouse a conventional behaviourist account of intelligence, describing it as 'the possession of a complex set of appropriate responses to the changing environment'.[11] Such a definition is interactionist, as befits an evolutionary outlook which sees intelligence as an instrument to help the organism to survive on a potentially hostile planet. Under the influence of a series of metaphors derived from ectopic thermodynamics and information theory, Churchland's conception of intelligence moves inwards until it becomes inscribed in the actual order or structure of the organism:

---

[11]   Paul Churchland (1988), p. 174.

> If the possession of information can be understood as the pos-
> session of some internal physical order that bears some system-
> atic relation to the environment, then the operation of
> intelligence, abstractly conceived, turns out to be just a high-
> grade version of the operating characteristics of life, save that
> they are even more intricately coupled to the environment . . .
> Intelligent life is just life, with a high thermodynamic intensity
> and an especially close coupling between internal order and
> external circumstance. (p. 174)

A system has intelligence inasmuch as

> it exploits the *information* it already contains, and the energy flux
> through it (this includes the energy flux through its sense
> organs), in such a way as to *increase* the information it contains.
> Such a system can *learn,* and it seems to be the central element of
> intelligence. (p. 173)

The 'especially close coupling between internal order and external circumstance' does not seem to be a distinctive feature of life;
according to the physicalist world picture within which
Churchland writes, it is the common condition of all existents.
Far from being the great achievement of life, one would have
thought that it was precisely the kind of thing that life — and
intelligent versions of it in particular — has been trying to
escape. So one is left with 'thermodynamic intensity' which, if it
means anything is the high level of information and negative
entropy which Churchland and others think is embodied in
*complex structures.

   We have already discussed the anthropomorphism inherent
in the use of *complex with reference to (unconscious) physical
systems. All systems (or tracts of matter) are, under the democratising eye of physics, equally complex or equally simple. (And
if this is the case, then the very notions of complexity and sim-
plicity — which are comparative, contrasting and interdepen-
dent terms — vanish). But what about the idea that there is
information implicit in systems, that *order is embodied information?* There are two types of problem with this very popular and
potently misleading belief. The first is a similar problem to that
associated with the term *complex: from the physicalist stand-
point, all pieces of matter are both random and highly ordered,
depending upon how, or at what level, they are viewed. Order,

ultimately, means explicit, visible or perceived order; and this, in turn, means order according to a human viewpoint. Without consciousness-born criteria of order (what shall count as ordered or as disordered), material entities are neither ordered nor disordered. (This is not to say that Man *imposes* order on an intrinsically disordered world; rather that he merely finds it *once it has been defined according to his criteria;* or, rather, he imposes order only to the extent that he imposes chaos).[12]

A rather different and even more serious criticism of the idea that the structure or internal physical order amounts to information (as if one's material assets can be capitilised as information flow) is that, quite apart from the dubious thermodynamics upon which the metaphor is founded, the structure of an organism is not available to it in the way that information is. It is certainly not part of consciousness. If one's structure *were* equal to information (about that structure?), then being a crystal would be a sufficient condition of being a crystallographer. A pebble's 'experience' may change its structure but that changed structure does not embody the experience. And the same applies to any organism where learning (and acquired information) is not thought to lead to conscious *memory. (The habit of conflating structural order and functional information is part of a larger tendency to fuse structural and occurrent memory. In a computer, and at a micro-anatomical level, it is not possible to make this distinction — which is why the use of *memory with respect to computers and bits of brain is invalid. But in real life the distinction is all-important: it is the difference between implicit and explicit past, implicit and explicit being there. This will be discussed further under MEMORY.)

Once information is uprooted from consciousness — and from an informant or from the experience of being informed and of wanting (or, come to that, refusing) to be informed — then any kind of nonsense is possible. According to the information theo-

[12] Even the most amorphous event or object can be analysed as if it were highly ordered. Fourier analysis presupposes that any time series can be analysed as the sum of (rhythmic) sinusoids of different frequencies. And the more amorphous it is, the more complex its analysis and, consequently, its apparent order.

rists we have discussed so far, the unconscious structure of organisms contains information and the energy impinging on the nervous system also contains information. It is possible to go further than this: for the fully paid up information theorist, information is simply and literally everywhere. The 'informationalisation' of the universe has been taken to its logical conclusion by theoreticians such as Fredkin, Toffoli and Wheeler[13] for whom the fundamental particles that make up the world — atoms, quarks, etc. — boil down to bits (binary digits) of information. The universe is composed of combinations of such binary digits; and atoms are 'information-processing systems'. The universe it seems is not only incredibly well-informed about itself — a huge polymath set out in boundless space, an infinity of omniscience — it *is* information. Fredkin's 'digital physics' has a further twist: it is based on the hypothesis that the universe no longer processes information like a computer but that it *is* a computer, still processing a programme that was installed at the beginning of time, possibly by a 'Great Programmer'. Whether or not this Computiverse is carried on the back of an elephant has not yet been determined.

The rationale behind this kind of thinking is clearly set out by Davies:

> Compare the activity of the computer with a natural physical system — for example, a planet going round the sun. The state of the system at any instant can be specified by giving the position and velocity of the planet. These are the input data. The relevant numbers can be given in binary arithmetic, as bit strings of ones and zeros. At some time later the planet will have a new position and velocity, which can be described by a new bit string: these are the output data. The planet has succeeded in converting one bit string into another, and is therefore in a sense a computer. The 'program' it has used in this conversion is a set of physical laws (Newton's laws of motion and gravitation).[14]

Physical systems are thus computational systems, processing information, just as computers do, and scientific laws may be

---

[13] The classic paper is Tommaso Toffoli's 'Physics and Computation' (1982).
[14] The best account of the 'computationalisation' of the universe is in Paul Davies *The Mind of God* (1993). The present discussion is particularly indebted to Chapter 5, 'Real Worlds and Virtual Worlds'.

considered as algorithms. This extraordinary view is apparently enhanced by the observation that in post-classical (quantum) physics many physical quantities normally regarded as continuous are in fact discrete: nature is thus more readily amenable to digitisation. In other words, the universe is not merely a huge computer: it is a huge *digital* computer. Digital physicists do not go so far as to say that it has an IBM operating system.

Some of the arguments surrounding digital physics are instructive — if only because they illustrate how completely consciousness can be overlooked. According to Wolfram:

> One expects the fact that computers are as powerful in their computational capacities as any physically realisable system can be, so that they can simulate any physical system. (Quoted in Davies, 1993, p. 119)

If this is true, then any physical system complex enough to compute can in principle simulate *the entire physical universe*. For those convinced so far, this raises an interesting question: if computers can mimic all physical systems, what distinguishes a simulated universe from the genuine article? The answer is even more interesting: nothing — once small problems of time-reversibility are overcome. For Fredkin, the entire universe *is* its own simulation — by a giant cellular automaton. Frank Tipler, who also believes this, counters the objection that the map (the simulation) is distinct from the territory (the universe) by asserting that this objection is valid only from a perspective outside of the computer. If the computer is powerful enough, it will encompass everything; there will be no outside and, for beings necessarily within the computer, the simulated world will be real.

As Davies points out, Tipler has to assume that a computer can simulate consciousness. Neither of them seems to regard this as a fatal flaw but it is. Consciousness cannot be simulated for two reasons: first, the Cartesian reason that it is enough to think that you are conscious to be conscious; and secondly, consciousness is logically prior to simulation — there have to be (deceived) human beings for a something (an event, an object, a state of affairs) to count *as* a simulation. Through these cracks, the light of common sense comes pouring in. In the absence of consciousness, physical events do not count as 'information' or 'information' processing. Nor do the laws of physics have *explicit* existence as 'algorithms' (which is not the same as saying that in the absence of consciousness the behaviour of the universe is un-law-like). Without consciousness, there are no data and no symbols. Even the classification of some events as 'inputs' and others as 'outputs' depends upon the assumption of a viewpoint, a reference point. Without the latter, there are neither inputs nor outputs: every event is potentially either and therefore intrinsically neither; for every exit is an entrance elsewhere.

Digital physics and the notion that the entire universe is composed of information or is a giant information processing system — that, according to Wheeler, It = Bit — is what lies at the end of a long chain of unchecked metaphors. Little by little, we arrive at lunacy. As is so often the case, the first steps on the path to lunacy appear innocuous. The most important and the seemingly most innocuous is that of accepting the idea that information can be 'stored' — outside of the human body, outside of conscious organisms — 'in' books or 'on' discs. In the loose sense of 'inform', I, who have derived a lot of information from a book I have read, may regard it as 'informative'. Likewise, a book I am writing may be informative; so (again, in a very loose sense) I am filling my book with information. The books I read inform me and the books I write are informed by me. Once the books are born, surely they can inform one another: information may be passed from book to book. Once this has been accepted, then information, informing and being informed start to be liberated from a *consciousness* being informed or wanting to inform. If it sounds odd to talk of one book informing another, consider what is often said about 'information stored on discs': information may be copied from one disc to another; information may be transmitted from disc to disc. This is perfectly normal computer talk; and it seems to suggest that information can be given and received without the involvement of consciousness. This is, of course, misleading: the information in a book, or on a disc, is only *potential* information. More generally, it is not information but only *potential information* that can be inscribed outside of a conscious organism. It remains potential until it is encountered by an individual requiring and able to receive information, able to be informed. In the absence of such a (conscious) organism, it is sloppy and inaccurate to refer to the states of objects as 'information'; but such loose talk is the beginning of a very long journey.

In conclusion, 'information' is absolutely pivotal to establishing the conceptual confusions so necessary to the seeming fruitfulness and explanatory power of much modern thought about the mind and the brain. By playing upon different meanings of the terms, it is possible to argue that minds, brains, organisms, various artifacts such as computers and even non-living thermodynamic systems are all information-processing devices. Because they are all essentially the same in this vitally important respect, they can be used to model each other; homology and analogy can run riot. Once the concept of information is liberated from the idea of *someone being informed* and from that of *someone doing the informing,* anything is possible.

INSTRUCTIONS

In computer terminology, an instruction is 'a set of bits or characters specifying an operation to be performed by the computer and identifying the data on which it is to be performed.'[15] A programme is a sequence of instructions. So far so good. As long as it is appreciated that the instructions in a computer are, ultimately, being issued by operators and that the computer is designed to carry out our, not its own, instructions, the anthropomorphism is harmless. For we must remember what a programme is: an explicit description of an effective procedure. And the latter is a procedure which reaches *a desired goal* in a finite number of steps using only a finite amount of knowledge. *We cannot separate the idea of an instruction from that of a desired goal and the latter must connect, however indirectly or remotely, with a desire.*

Problems begin when this is forgotten and we start to think of computers as issuing their own instructions; or when, extending computer terminology beyond computers, we begin to talk (and presumably think) of naturally occurring objects as issuing

[15]   Darcy and Boston (1984).

instructions. For example, it is often said that DNA is a set of instructions for building an organism. Dawkins describes the process of evolution thus:

> The nonrandom survival and reproductive success of individuals within the species effectively 'writes' improved instructions for survival into the collective genetic memory of the species as the generations go by. (Dawkins, 1988, p. 119)

It is significant that 'writes' is in inverted commas but not 'instructions'.

So long as the metaphorical status of 'instructions' — outside of its application to human beings or to artifacts understood as acting on their behalf — is appreciated, no harm will result. If it is not appreciated, we are on the road to rampant anthropomorphism.

INTERPRETATION (TRANSLATION)

> A central problem of perception is how the brain interprets the patterns of the eye in terms of external objects. (Gregory, 1970, p. 15)

In everyday terms, interpretation is making sense of something one has encountered — seen, heard, read, etc. — as a result of which one understands it, or understands it better. Interpretation is a fundamental activity of human consciousness. There is a narrower everyday use of 'interpretation': translation from one language to another or from a code into a language one understands. This narrower sense is rooted in the primary meaning of making sense (for oneself or for others) of something, or of making better sense of it.

There is a computational sense of interpretation which is not necessarily, and certainly not necessarily directly, related to understanding and consciousness. The interpreter in a computer is a programme that translates each statement in a source programme into machine language, executes it, and repeats the process for each new statement until the entire programme has been executed.'[16] No consciousness is necessary and conscious understanding does not result. This difference between ordi-

---

[16]   Darcy and Boston (1984).

nary and computational senses of 'interpretation' is fundamental. There are, of course, points of similarity between human and computational interpreters and between everyday and computational senses of interpretation. The most important of these seems to be that some human interpretation (language translation) and, apparently, all computational interpretation involves the replacement of one group of symbols by another. But this does not close the gap between human and machine interpretation. Replacing French symbols by English is not the same as understanding a statement in French (or in English). Searle demonstrated this with his famous 'Chinese room' argument.[17] He envisaged an individual ignorant of Chinese provided with a set of Chinese symbols and a set of rules for using them. Such an individual could respond to an input of Chinese symbols with a correct output without knowing the meaning of either input or output.

That the replacement of one (input) symbol by another (output) symbol in accordance with an algorithm does *not* amount to interpretation in the ordinary sense of the word is less obvious than it might be because of the anthropomorphic resonance of terms like symbol. If we describe the substitution by a computer of one symbol by another as 'interpretation', it is very difficult not to think of the symbols meaning something to the computer. If, moreover, we think of the meaning (and reference) of the symbol as its causal relations, this attribution of meaning acquisition to computational interpretation becomes irresistible. Of course, it remains invalid: the computer does not have semantics because the symbols remain uninterpreted: the passage from one (uninterpreted) symbol to another (uninterpreted) symbol does not count as interpretation. (I am not even sure that, in the absence of semantics, it can be considered as having syntax, except in a narrow, technical sense. It is difficult to see how one can allocate terms to parts of speech in the absence of knowing what they mean.) The input relations of its symbols do not confer semantic content upon them and the causally downstream events in the peripherals are not their meaning, either.

---

[17]   The 'Chinese room' argument was first set out in Searle (1980).

When we read, therefore, that: 'The instructions of the universal [Turing] machine enable it to interpret the instructions
encoded in the binary numeral, and to carry them out on the
data';[18] or that 'RNA interprets the instructions encoded in
DNA', we should be on our guard.

LANGUAGE (CODE)

The ubiquitous misuse of these ubiquitous terms has contrib-
uted almost as much as the misuse of 'information' to the present
state of happy conceptual confusion in contemporary psychology. We hear of 'languages' of the brain and of nervous systems
and DNA 'encoding' information. We learn that computers use
and somehow seem to speak 'computer languages'. In the ordinary run of things, language is something used by a conscious
person to convey information or other sorts of meanings to
another conscious person. In the world of computer-speak,
languages may be spoken fluently by non-conscious entities
such as laptop computers, single neurons and nucleoproteins.

The preference for the term 'code' over language is revealing,
suggesting a certain amount of embarrassment with the suggestion that computers and neurons and large molecules are chatty.
It should not relieve any embarrassment, of course, because
codes are secondary developments from languages and
dependent upon them. Morse code users are more, not less
sophisticated, than ordinary speakers; for in order to be able to
use morse code, one has to understand the first order language
(such as English) which it encodes as well as the second-order
language (morse) in which it is encoded. The attraction of the
term 'code' is that the elements, like those of morse, do not make
immediate sense: they are remote from the terms used in ordinary languages. And a code has a highly formalised, explicit
*grammar. We are therefore more inclined to believe that DNA
speaks fluent morse than that it speaks English (with or without
a Northern accent).

A couple of related terms that are used with particular fre-
quency in cognitive scientology are 'signal' and 'symbol'. In

[18]   Johnson-Laird (1988), p. 5l.

everyday life, signals are events that have meaning to conscious organisms; and they are typically emitted by conscious organisms in order to convey meaning, though they may be read without being written. In cognitive science, signals are found at much lower levels. For example, clusters of nerve impulses — even where they occur in parts of the brain that are not thought to be conscious or related to consciousness — are described as signals (or messages). Indeed, for Patricia Churchland, 'the distinctive thing about neurons is that they are instruments of communication', receiving and emitting signals.[19] Of course, the brain does not signal in English; it talks to itself in code. The events in the nervous system encode events in the world — and hence the world itself. Gregory tells us that

> What the eye does is to feed the brain with *information coded into neural activity — chains of electrical impulses — which by their code and the *patterns of brain activity represent objects. (Gregory, 1974, p. 9)

The code is sometimes rather Byzantine; for example the activation of a certain group of neurones at a certain intensity will constitute a point in a taste space and hence encode a particular taste. Or would, if there were someone to decode it.

According to Johnson-Laird, all mental representations are 'symbols'; it is 'a major tenet of cognitive science that the mind is a symbolic system' and 'perception leads to the construction of mental symbols *representing the world . . . nerve impulses and other electrochemical events can therefore be treated as the underlying primitives — perhaps analog in form — out of which the symbols are constructed.'[20]

LEVEL

Everyone can see that a thought is different from the passsage of ions through semi-permeable membranes and that a friend is more than a collection of molecules. And yet, according to physicalists, and, in particular, identity theorists, the thought and the passage of ions, the friend and the collection of mole-

---

[19]   Patricia Churchland (1986), p. 48.
[20]   Johnson-Laird (1988), p. 35.

cules are the same thing. This apparent paradox and apparently
fatal weakness of physicalism is overcome by appealing to the
notion of 'levels'. The friend and the collection of molecules, the
thought and the passage of ions through semi-permeable membranes are the same things — but *observed or described at different
levels*. To cite an analogy often invoked in support of the 'levels'
argument, a picture in a newspaper is at one level just a collection of dots of different shades of black and at another a representation of, say, a face. So what is at one level merely a
collection of molecules is, at another, a conscious human being.
An entity that is a mindless collection of material particles when
observed at the molecular level may be the intelligible basis of
consciousness at another. The transition from one level to
another is sufficient to explain the emergence of consciousness.

The levels argument is inadmissible. The reason very briefly is
this. When we talk about levels, we are, at least implicitly, talking about levels of *appearance,* or of *representation,* or of *description.* Different levels of appearance, representation or description cannot explain consciousness, or its emergence from matter
considered to be essentially and intrinsically unconscious,
because levels etc. *presuppose* consciousness, *presuppose* a viewpoint upon the object in question.

The levels argument is so widely invoked (either implicitly or
explicitly) that it is unnecessary to give chapter and verse. I shall
confine myself to a couple of exemplary instances. The
neuroscientist Szenthagothai writes:

> Although distributed over large parts of the brain (not exclu-
> sively the cortex), the reflective level of the mind has the same
> material substrate as the brain, the only difference being that
> while ordinary brain functions can occur in separate, even
> rather small, portions of the nervous system, the reflective level
> (or mind) is a global function of all or most of the central nervous
> system. There is thus no gap to be bridged as regards the neural
> substrate of mind: the problem is only how anything emerging
> on the reflective level can act back upon the neural level.
> (Szenthagothai, 1987)

'The reflective level' is 'a global function of all or most of the
nervous system in two senses: it is dependent upon the nervous
system acting as a whole; and it is something that the nervous

system as a whole can do or bring about — something the parts are not capable of'.

Levels not only have an existence independent of any observing consciousness — so they are out there in material unconscious things — but they have, apparently, causal efficacy. Or at least according to John Searle they do.[21] Searle tries to reconcile his biological naturalism (the view that 'mental states are as real as any other biological phenomena' and are caused by and cause biological phenomena) with the fact that mental states are totally different from physical ones. He does this by stating that 'mental states are both *caused by* and *realised in* the structure of the brain (and the rest of the central nervous system).' (p. 265) This is precisely comparable, he claims, to the way in which 'the liquid properties of water are both *caused by* the molecular behaviour and *realised in* the collection of molecules'. The analogy leads Searle into some very muddy waters indeed:

> So if one asked, 'How can there be a causal relation between the molecular behaviour and the liquidity if the same stuff is both liquid and a collection of molecules?', the answer is that there can be causal relations between phenomena at different levels in the very same underlying stuff.

An entity or stuff can causally interact with itself in virtue of being seen at two levels!

It is worth spelling out what is wrong with Searle's argument because, although fallacious, it is not particularly unorthodox. It is the logical outcome of the unthinking use of levels in discussions about the relationships between mind and brain, between thoughts and ionic movements, and between persons and molecules.

First of all, there is something profoundly suspicious about the analogy (never mind the homology):

Brain states : Mental states :: Molecular behaviour : Liquidity

It implies that the relation between the physical and the mental is similar to the relationship between one type of experience of the physical and another, between one way of being conscious of, or describing, a physical entity and another. This seems odd

---

[21] See Searle (1983), Chapter 10.

because both the molecules and the liquidity of the water are on the same side of the mind–matter divide: either on the matter side if they are thought of as intrinsic properties of material water; or on the mind side if they are thought of as different ways of experiencing or observing water.

Secondly, it suggests that there can be causal relations between these types of experiences or levels of description. 'It is tempting', Searle says, 'to think that whenever A causes B there must be two discrete events, one identified as cause, the other as effect'. But this temptation must be resisted: events at a macro level are caused by events at a micro level; so one can get out of two levels all that one has hitherto wanted to get out of two separate events. In the case of the mind/brain, the levels are apportioned as follows: 'The intrinsically *mental* features of the universe are just higher level *physical* features of brains.'[22]

The notion of the causal interaction between mind and body as being essentially the same as a causal interaction between descriptions is rather obscure. Searle believes, it seems, that when matter acts upon mind (to alter mental states) and mind acts on matter (to bring about intentions), it is a question of one description of a system acting upon another — as if the level of description of the system were not only part of the system (which of course it is not) but also enabled that system to interact with itself. Without such levels of description, or observation, one must presume, matter could not give rise to mind nor mind act upon matter. This confusion of descriptions with objects described is even more spectacular than Hacker's witty analogy with 'buildings talking to one another in the language of classical architecture'.[23]

Searle's talk of levels takes the 'transferred epithet' approach to the mind/brain problem one step further: we have transferred descriptions!

[22] Searle (1987), p. 225.
[23] Hacker (1987), p. 487.

LOGIC

Since time immemorial, logic has been associated with consciousness and logical operations regarded as distinct achievements of consciousness at its most developed and sophisticated. Man may not be the only rational animal but he is unique in the degree to which he engages in explicitly logical thought. This uniqueness is denied by some and we are frequently asked to believe that nonconscious machines, or even parts of machines, carry out logical operations and that logical operations may be carried out in the lower reaches of the brain without surfacing in consciousness. Logical operations may be executed without consciousness. This, it is believed, has momentous consequences for the philosophy of mind. According to Dennett,[24] the development of modern computers has taken away the force of Descartes' argument that reasoning betokens a non-physical substance.

There are several strands in this conception of logic disassociated from consciousness. Each deserves separate critical inspection.

(1) Logic is in machines

Electronic engineers and computer experts talk about 'logic circuits' and 'logic gates'. Such talk is clearly anthropomorphic. A NAND gate does not, of itself, execute logical operations. It requires a conscious individual to turn this input/output relation

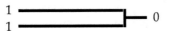

into a logical operation corresponding to 'not (A and B)'. And the same applies to more complex logical operations, even those conducted by 'expert systems' in natural language. The electronic events within the machine count as logical operations only if they are understood as relations between inputs and outputs that are themselves understood i.e. interpreted by a conscious human operator.

---

[24] Dennett (1986).

(2) *There are logic circuits in the brain*

Parts of the brain are spoken of as if they were organic computers ('wetware') executing logical operations. We are told that
there are 'logic gates' in the spinal cord and the cerebellum;
if-then circuits in the cortex; and so on. This is a particularly
complex mess to unravel. It seems to involve three steps:

a)   'machinomorphic' attitudes to brain; the brain thought
     of as a kind of device, as if it were an artifact that had been
     made with some purpose in view;

b)   the anthropomorphising of machines in line with *(1)*
     above;

c)   the application of the anthropomorphised conception of
     machines to the de-anthropomorphised brain, so that its
     operations can be termed 'logical' and its neuronal
     elements logic circuits.

(3) *The mind is a kind of logic machine*

According to Patricia Churchland, 'the mind is a kind of logic
machine that operates on sentences.'[25] The concept of machine is
brought right into the heart of mind: logic and mind are reunited
but no consciousness results or is necessary. Mind-logic remains
machine-logic. This position is the end-point of a bio-logic which
derives ultimately from Helmholtz, who first suggested that
perception was based upon 'unconscious inference'. For many
cognitive psychologists, perceptions are inferences from sensory
and stored data or the result of inference mechanisms operating
on sensory '*information'.[26] According to Richard Gregory:

> To understand perception, the signal codes and the stored
> knowledge or assumptions used for deriving perceptual
> hypotheses must be discovered . . . perceptions are inferences
> based on signalled data from the senses and stored in memory.
> (quoted in Shanker, 1986, p. 228)

The fundamental error behind the machine-bio-logic claim is
that it fails to distinguish between conscious reasoning, which
may be quite effortful, and events that may have the same appar-

---

[25]   Patricia Churchland (1986), p. 252.
[26]   For a comprehensive critical review of this notion, see Shanker (1986).

ent input–output relations as conscious reasoning but are not even effortless. The logic of the logic-circuit is not strictly logic because the events have been totally uprooted from — and in fact never bore any relation to — the process of reasoning, the business of being reasonable. We may use machines to assist us to draw logical inferences but it is we, not the machines, that draw the inferences. The output of a machine is no more an inference than natural processes are inferences: without explicitness, without consciousness, there are events but no true logical operations.

Of course, we can attribute our own intentionality to the machines we devise for our own purposes, in the same way as we can regard a cloud as a standing assertion to the effect that it is probably going to rain. Likewise, when one stone falls on another and the second stone is broken in two, we could regard this as a valid calculation to the effect that $1 + 1 = 1 + \frac{1}{2} + \frac{1}{2}$ or even an invalid calculation to the effect that $1 + 1 = 3$. In either case, we are committing the error — common in cognitive science — of *misplaced explicitness.

MEMORY (STORED INFORMATION)

Computers, we are told, have memories as well as logic; and so it doesn't seen unreasonable that we can use computers to model minds which, importantly, have memories. Now there are many senses in which it is roughly true to say that computers have memories — *but there are many others in which it is not at all true.* In its original and true sense, memory is inseparable from consciousness; in an extended sense, it is separable from but closely serves consciousness; and, in a greatly extended, metaphorical sense, memory has nothing to do with consciousness. The neuroscience ploy is to apply the term in its metaphoric, unconscious sense to machines, brains-considered-as-machines, organisms, and even to non-living non-artifactual matter, and then to gloss over the differences between this sense and the primary, stricter, sense of memory — the sense which gathers up the really interesting and mysterious aspects of the phenomenon.

The primary sense of memory corresponds to occurrent or episodic memory: conscious memory for particular facts or events which may be recalled involuntarily or at will — in either case explicitly. Amongst these are personal or autobiographical memories that relate to things that one has oneself experienced. In the case of such memories one often recalls not only the event but the fact that one was there to witness it. The recollection is imbued with a sense of a past self. The memories are explicitly past *experiences;* they are related consciously to one's self and to a past which is one's own and for which one feels in part responsible.

Other senses of memory are less directly related to consciousness, less rooted in recalled past experience. Procedural memories (remembering how to do something), acquired skills which one may deploy more or less consciously, habit memories (behaving differently as a result of past experience), may be retained independently of any accessible episodic memory. There are many forms of amnesia in which it is possible to learn new skills without acquiring new occurrent memories. In such cases, the individual is unable to recall anything about the circumstances in which the new skill was acquired. Such pathological cases dramatise the difference between procedural and occurrent memory. The past may be active in the present even though one may not explicitly recall it.

This distinction is, perversely, used to licence the complete separation of memory from consciousness and the further extension of the term 'memory' to encompass the enduring effect of any event upon any object — as if procedural memory were the real thing and occurrent, episodic or declarative memory an unimportant sub-type. If I fall over and cut myself badly, a scar will form which may remain with me for the rest of my life. This scar is a record of the event that caused it and, by preserving it intact, my body has, in a sense, 'remembered' the event, long after *I* have forgotten it. The general notion is that, if an event causes a permanent change in an object, that change is a memory of the event, 'stored *information' about it: the permanent change has stored the past. In this extended sense, all sorts of naturally occurring stuff has — or is — memory. For example, DNA. Or a rock bearing the marks of an ante-diluvian geological catastrophe.

It is worth teasing out the logic here. If order is *information and memory is the transmission of *information over time, any ordered system that endures will seem to have, or to be, memory. Of course, once the concept of memory is extended to include any permanent change that has taken place as the result of the impact of an event, or the interaction between objects, then memory is everywhere: the present state of the universe could be seen to be a continually changing memory of the entire past of the universe. And the more inert the universe, the more it would appear to be saturated with, or identical with, memory.[27] The most impressive feats of memory will be exhibited by rocks that do not alter over many millions of years.

It will be obvious that something has gone wrong. If the sense of memory has been so extended that it now includes the entire state of the universe — irrespective, moreover, of whether it has any conscious inhabitants — then it has no meaning distinct from stability or, as I have said, from inertia. This result lies at the bottom of a slope at the top of which is the decision to separate the concept of memory from that of consciousness. This is a perfectly acceptable move, so long as it is not then forgotten that memory now has several distinct meanings and that memory without consciousness is a rather specialised meaning, the metaphorical extension of a term whose primary meaning is connected with consciousness.

The primacy of conscious memory — and in particular of autobiographical occurrent memory — is demonstrated by the fact that those in whom this is defective though all other aspects of memory are intact are regarded as profoundly amnesic and severely impaired. Germane to this primary sense are deliberate and conscious recall, the savouring of memories, reminiscence and nostalgia. These aspects of human memory are not minor or optional characteristics. For they are connected with the central fact of personal memory: its being rooted in the sense that 'this

---

[27] The analogy with what follows when the concept of *information is uprooted from consciousness, from individuals giving and receiving *information, will be obvious.

happened to me', 'this memory is about me', 'this is *my* memory'. Moreover, true memory is implicated in our sense of the present: the familiarity of objects and of the world and its feeling of being related to me and I to it.

Until such time as computers, or DNA, or elastic show convincing signs of nostalgia, we should be on our guard whenever we hear that they have, or encode, or embody[28] memories. They may help us to recall things but they do not themselves remember their 'memories'. In this regard, there is no metaphysical difference between an interactive laser disc and a knotted handkerchief. They are not so much memories as reminders; and they are able to remind only those who actually have memories in the real, primary sense.

(We should be equally guarded when we encounter the term 'memory store' or '*stored information'. Of the making and occurrence of databases there is, it appears, no end. But the concept of stored *information is only a useful shorthand and it should not be taken literally. While it is in store it is not actually *information: '*information' that is not informing anyone is not *information. See INFORMATION).

As an example of just how muddled neuro-computational cognitive psychology can be on the topic of memory, the following is worth pondering:

> Despite their limitations, simple auto-associative memories show many of the valuable properties of neural computation. What they remember is the pattern of activity created across their units by the external input. All learning rules store some aspect of the pairwise co-occurrence statistics in the units in the weightings on their connections. (Phillips, 1988, p. 392)

MISPLACED EXPLICITNESS

There are things that we do (deliberately, explicitly) and things that happen. The abiding mystery of conscious human beings is that they are able to create doing out of happening, to fashion

---

[28] The equivocation here is instructive. We are told that DNA is 'stored information', is genetic memory. It does not, however, have this memory. It does not remember; it *is* 'memory'. When I remember, I do not become my memories; I have them. This distance is an essential part of memory in its true, that is to say human, sense.

agency out of agent-less event, to carve choice out of the unchosen, deliberation out of mechanism. Thus, my deliberately going for a walk is predicated upon a complex hierarchy of reflexes necessary for directed ambulation. *I* walk, yes, but *it* provides the walking mechanisms; I do walking, but I do not 'do' the modulation of vestibulo-spinal tone necessary to permit walking to take place.

One result of the inversion of the hierarchy of mental phenomena (so that calculations are at the bottom and sensations at the top) noted in the discussion of *calculations is that deliberate operations, displaced from the higher reaches of the mind as the latter are computerised, reappear surprisingly at lower levels. Consider Johnson-Laird on vision:

> Your visual system constructs a description of the perceived object and compares it with some sort of mental catalogue of the three-dimensional shape of objects. It can recognise them from particular viewpoints and then make automatic extrapolations about the rest of their shapes. (Johnson-Laird, 1988, p. 114)

This sounds a jolly sight more difficult than simply seeing the object and recognising it! Johnson-Laird's account illustrates how, when explicitness and deliberation have been displaced from the places where it is usually considered to be — ordinary behaviour — they reappear elsewhere in the *mechanisms* postulated to underlie ordinary behaviour. The terminology appropriate to conscious, indeed higher-order conscious, activity also re-appears — precisely where, *ex hypothesi*, consciousness should be absent. That it *should* be absent is evident from Johnson-Laird's own assertion (on the same page of his book) that 'the machinery of [visual] identification is unconscious in the Helmholtzian sense'.

Whenever you try to drive out consciousness from the places where it is ordinarily thought to be, from its rightful place, it will return in places where it obviously has no right to be — the only genuine example, perhaps, of Freud's 'return of the repressed'!

PATTERN

The appeal to 'patterns' is rather like the appeal to 'levels': both are invoked to help explain how an entity such as the nervous system whose elements are very simple and unquestionably material can give rise to something — the mind — that is apparently neither. All nerve impulses are roughly the same; they differ only in the *patterns* they form which can encode the extraordinary variety of the perceived world. These patterns emerge at a higher *level.

The points made in relation to level apply *a fortiori* here: patterns are viewpoint-dependent. To illustrate this, consider the following diagram, intended to represent an array of neurones in a state of excitation:

$$\begin{matrix} \bullet & \bullet & \bullet & \bullet \\ \bullet & \bullet & \bullet & \bullet \\ \bullet & \bullet & \bullet & \bullet \end{matrix}$$

What is the pattern of activity here? It could be read as

$$\begin{matrix} \bullet & \bullet & \bullet & \bullet \\ \bullet & \bullet & \bullet & \bullet \\ \bullet & \bullet & \bullet & \bullet \end{matrix}$$

or as

$$\bullet \; \bullet \; \bullet \; \bullet \quad + \quad \bullet \; \bullet \; \bullet \; \bullet \quad + \quad \bullet \; \bullet \; \bullet \; \bullet$$

or as

$$\begin{matrix} \bullet \; \bullet & & \bullet \; \bullet \\ \bullet \; \bullet & + & \bullet \; \bullet \\ \bullet \; \bullet & & \bullet \; \bullet \end{matrix}$$

or as a collection of six pairs. The truth is that, from an array of activated neurones, any number of potential patterns could be extracted. *Which* of these is *the* pattern of activity is an unanswerable question. Intrinsically, from the physicalist point of view that neuroscientists espouse, it is none of these: a consciousness, a viewpoint, is required in order to decide between possible patterns; in order that one pattern rather than another should emerge victorious; in order that there should be *any* pattern. If the nervous system is to be viewed as a physico-chemical system, as something that has no viewpoint, then the events in it have no more intrinsic pattern than do the events in a stone, or an avalanche. In short, the emergence of specific patterns is dependent upon consciousness; they cannot, therefore, explain the origin or emergence of consciousness.

PROCESS (PROCESSING)

For the thinker bluffing his way across the brain/mind barrier, travelling is always easier to handle than arrival. Despite the alternate machinisation and anthropomorphisation of terms, it still sometimes remains difficult to deal with them when they approximate old-fashioned unreconstructed consciousness. Even *information can embarrass; so, instead, arrival is replaced by further journeying and writers sometimes prefer to talk about 'information processing' rather than 'information'. Consciousness is thus sufficiently distanced from self-presence to be convincingly machinised. So seeing becomes 'optical information processing';[29] and neurons are 'information-processing devices'.[30] Indeed, we are often told that the brain is an information processor of almost incredible complexity'.[31] This conventional view is endorsed fulsomely by Johnson-Laird, who is very concerned to ensure that journeying displaces arrival entirely:

> What do mental processes *process?* The answer, of course, is a vast number of perceptions, ideas, images, beliefs, hypotheses, thoughts and memories. One of the tenets of cognitive science is that all these entities are mental representations or symbols of one sort or another. (Johnson-Laird, 1988, p. 28)

The very things that we would regard as the contents of (conscious) mind — ideas, thoughts, memories, etc. — are relegated to the material that is processed — by mental processes. There is raw material and processing (starting point and journeying) but

---

[29]   Paul Churchland (1988), p. 114.
[30]   Paul Churchland (1988), p. 133.
[31]   Longuet-Higgins (1988).

no product (arrival). The mind is more convincingly machine-like if, like machines, it does jobs rather than being composed of mental states. For example, the following is seemingly more convincing for being about '*information processing' than about mental states:

> Information processing is achieved in neural systems by a large number of highly interconnected units that affect each other's levels of activation through broadcast signals that are modified at the receiving end by local connection strengths. The dynamic change of activation under the influence of external input, current state, and internal connections constitutes information processing, and modifications of the connections constitutes learning. (Phillips, 1988, p. 392)

This emphasis upon processing rather than upon products also makes it easier to identify mental phenomena with nerve impulses which also exist in travel rather than arrival.

Finally, there are useful ambiguities in the idea of 'information processing': is it a question of turning something that is not information into information; or is it a matter of turning one sort of information into another sort? These uncertainties stop one looking too closely and asking what form information — or information processing — takes in neural terms.

Examples of information processing often revolve around the events that take place at a synapse — the junction between two neurones — where two subthreshold pre-synaptic excitatory impulses add up to one that actually breaks threshold to cross the synaptic cleft, or where two impulses, one excitatory and the other inhibitory, partially cancel one another out. But is one entitled to think of this as the processing (production/transformation/enhancement) of information? After all, convergence of 'signals' at a synapse may be equally regarded as loss, rather than use, or gain, of information. If the central pathways know only the result of the convergence of incoming activity at synapses they have lost access to the components that made it up. If we are given answer '4', we do not know what elements went into that result: 2 + 2 or 3 + 1.

In short, we have no idea how energy is turned into information and fudging the issue by talking about 'information *process-*

ing' does not help, either — except insofar as it unfocusses the question and makes it easier to enjoy the illusion that one is answering it.

REPRESENTATION (MODEL)

Careers have been built upon 'representation' and upon 'model'. 'Representation' is a key term in *Fodorese and, indeed, throughout cognitive psychology. The roots of its current usage are philosophical, though within cognitive psychology it has taken on a life of its own. According to Johnson-Laird: 'One of the tenets of cognitive science is that all the entities are mental representations.'[32]

Representationalist theories of the mind begin with the claim that we do not have direct access to external reality, only to mental representations of reality. What we have contact with is not, say, the surface of objects, but a mental event or content caused by the external object. Representationalist theories of the mind follow naturally from the causal, interactionist, theory of perception, according to which perception (and hence consciousness) is, or is the result of, the *effect* the external world has on a specialised part of the body, namely the nervous system. The question then arises as to what form the representations of the world in the mind (or the nervous system) take. The naive assumption is that the mind mirrors the world; or, at the very least, the mental phenomenon has some feature in common with the object or property it is about, for example a common form, so that the mental phenomenon is *isomorphic* with the physical object it relates to. This view quickly runs into difficulties, though, as we shall see, thinkers are drawn back to it again and again. Since the representation of the object is the result of an *interaction* between the object and the nervous system, it cannot simply look like the object. This was pointed out by Helmholtz, who, unfortunately, went on to suggest that the events in the nervous system were *symbols* of external reality.

Contemporary representationalism in psychology may be traced to the immediate post-War writings of Kenneth Craik,

---

[32] Johnson-Laird (1988), p. 28.

who took the idea of symbols further and suggested that the mind or the nervous system constructed a *model* of reality out of these symbols: external reality is known to us because it is reconstructed or symbolically represented within our nervous systems/minds. We have direct access not to the world but to transforms, models, representations of it. This view, now ubiquitous throughout cognitive psychology (whose commitment to mental representation is what distinguishes it from the old, despised behaviourism), philosophical psychology and artificial intelligence, achieved its most elaborate recent expression — indeed its apotheosis — in Johnson-Laird's *Mental Models* (1983).

The main and the most obvious criticism of the representational or model theory of mind is that it raises the homunculus problem. To what or whom are the representations representing (re-presenting) the world? This is particularly obvious if mental models are thought to be pictures in the mind: who or what is going to look at them? For pictures imply spectators and, indeed, spectators able to interpret their elements, translating them into the elements of the depicted object or state of affairs. This difficulty is equally obvious (despite a considerable amount of fast footwork) if the representations are propositions cast in some postulated 'language of thought' — in, for example, Fodor's Mentalese; for the language of thought seems to require someone to whom it is addressed and who will also interpret its symbols. If representations are neither of these homunculus-generating things, then it is difficult to know what they are.

For Johnson-Laird,[33] who distances himself from both the image and the proposition versions of representationalism, they are 'internal tableaux'. These, however, seem to require homunculi to use them at least as much as images and propositions do. Despite strenuous denials, the homunculus problem cannot be driven away from representational theories of mind. Indeed, it becomes more apparent the more representationalists try to wriggle away from it. Johnson-Laird asserts that

> unlike a propositional representation, a mental model does not
> have an arbitrarily chosen syntactic structure, but one that plays

---

[33]   See Johnson-Laird (1983), Chapter 3 'What Mental Models Are Not'.

a direct representational role since it is analogous to the corresponding state of affairs — as we perceive, so we conceive. (Johnson-Laird, 1983, p. 156)

The structure of mental models 'is identical to the structure of states of affairs'. This claimed isomorphism seems to solve, or dissolve, the homunculus problem by the following logic: if the mental model is structurally identical to the state of affairs it models, it will self-evidently be about that state of affairs and will require no further interpretation; if the model requires no further interpretation, it will not require the consciousness of an homunculus for whom it is a model in order to be a model. The second claim does not, of course, follow from the first: a transparent model requires an homunculus just as urgently as does one requiring more active interpretation. The homunculus doesn't have to be so clever — a thick homunculus will do — but he/she is still needed.

It is clear that, as mentioned already, naive mirror representationalism remains a perpetual temptation, often taking the form of a proposed isomorphism between the physical and the mental, between the external objects and the internal ones.[34] This raises two new problems: how, for example, yellow could be represented isomorphically in the nervous system by non-yellow phenomena; and how that representation is itself consciousness or is presented in consciousness. The first question is often answered by claiming that the different properties of the outside world are represented by 'sites in vector space'. According to Paul Churchland, 'activity vectors form the most important kind of representation within the brain.'[35] But this 'coding' dodge reintroduces the problem of decoding and the question of how the representation is 'understood'. The second question leads to a retreat from representationalism altogether in the hope of abolishing the homunculus problem. Johnson-Laird's transparent (because isomorphic) representations may represent a half-way retreat from representationalism. It has been characterised by James Russell as follows: 'mental models aren't

---

[34] For a discussion of isomorphism see Tallis (1991), the section 'Exhibiting Consciousness' in Chapter 8.

[35] Paul Churchland (1988), p. 165.

just representations. Why, they're the real thing . . . though still mental, of course.'[36] Despite these insuperable difficulties (and the fact that representationalism solves no problems itself or even provides a framework for solving problems), its intuitive attractiveness makes it irresistible. For it provides a framework within which the real problems can be by-passed and the illusion of progress maintained. Yates' review begins by suggesting that the central claim of cognitive psychology 'is that information about the world is coded in the form of mental representations that are distinct from external information and sensory information.'[37] He argues that 'the content of awareness consists of constructs that account for sensations by representing patterns of the environment relevant to the set of possible actions that might be taken.' The data upon which these constructs are based do not correspond solely to sensations: perceptions are representations of the world that are incompletely accounted for by what reaches the sensorium from the world. The models that constitute our awareness are based upon centrally directed inference from sensation.

Such a direct identification of models or representations with awareness is particularly embarrassing to those who would avoid the homunculus problem. There are several ways out. Johnson-Laird, writing several years after *Mental Models*, talks of 'implicit representations' : 'The brain itself may represent much of its knowledge in an implicit representation based on parallel distributed *processing.'[38] An implicit representation is, presumably, one that no-one in particular is explicitly conscious of: it doesn't represent anything to anyone. Once we admit the possibility of implicit representations, then representations may be found anywhere. The universal *grammar of human language may be represented in the brain of a new-born child. Truth tables may be represented in the logic circuits of a pocket computer.

---

[36] Russell (1986). This is by far the best account I have come across of the problems of contemporary representationalism in psychology and the various ploys that have been used in an endeavour to kill off the homunculus.

[37] Yates (1985), p. 249.

[38] Johnson-Laird (1988), p. 389.

The instructions for making an organism — genetic information — may be represented in its DNA. *Rules may be represented in unconscious computational systems. Newton's laws of motion may be represented in planetary orbits. And so on.

The fundamental flaw in representationalist thought is that it overlooks the primary sense of representation — that of re-presentation. A picture is a representation of something that may in its own right be present. Representation is secondary to presentation — to presence — and thus requires consciousness. It is an indirect presentation — via signs — of *something to someone*. Things are represented to — just as they are presented to — consciousnesses. *A representation cannot therefore be the basis of, but presupposes, consciousness.* And for this reason, the description of something as a 'representation' in the absence of a consciousness to or for which it represents — unless it is explicitly acknowledged that a consciousness is potentially there — should arouse suspicion. 'Unconscious representation' is a deviant form and should prompt vigilance. At the risk of labouring the point: there can be no re-presentation without presentation.

Since presentation itself presupposes presence, i.e. consciousness, consciousness cannot be founded upon representation, cannot be seen as emerging effortlessly from modelling of the world, understood as the generation of internal transforms of the world within, say, a nervous system. Presentations presuppose someone — a consciousness — to whom the presentation is presented, to whom, at least, it is *present*. Without that someone, or that consciousness, it is difficult to know by what right the object or entity counts as a presentation, or a re-presentation.

In the topsy-turvy world of cognitive psychology, we are allowed to speak of representations in the absence of consciousness — though representations require consciousness — and to speak of consciousness as a set of representations — though consciousness is the terminus at which representation gives way to presentation, to presence. Some explanation of this craziness is necessary. It lies, perhaps, in the ambiguities of 'representation'. Let us look at a couple of these:

(1) It is acceptable to say that pictures represent things — but only because it is assumed that they are being looked at by some-

one. By itself, a picture is simply an object and lacks intentional reference to any other object. At best it is a *potential* representation of something. We tend to forget this seemingly pedantic requirement and, as a result, think of the picture itself as a 'representation'. This paves the way for thinking of other things — nerve impulses etc. — as being able to represent things and so becoming the basis of consciousness or of a model of consciousness.

(2) Cognitive scientists often frame their fundamental question as follows: 'How is the world represented in the brain?' This is open to two interpretations: what representation (image etc.) does the world have in the brain (or what transforms of its image are in the brain?); and in what form is it present in the brain? To underline the ambiguity of the question, compare the two ways in which the Pope may be represented: through a picture; or through a representative, a legate. Representation in the first sense allows a meaningful incorporation of the world into the brain. This, however, raises the homunculus problem — since meaning has to mean to someone, pictures have to depict for someone. Representation in the second sense closes off the homunculus series; for the representative is a kind of terminus. A legate is not a picture and is in himself a terminus.[39] Such an ambiguity keeps representationalism alive.

RULE

An entire family of anthropomorphic terms gathers round this word. It is particularly useful for assisting the passage across the mind/ brain, mind/matter barrier, since following a rule, which is something that conscious creatures do, also seems to be something — like conforming to a law — that unconscious entities are capable of. Rule-following, that is to say, has one foot in mechanism and one in deliberation.

Cognitive psychologists and others would have us believe that:

---

[39] Szenthagothai's definition of mind — 'the level of representation of wholeness, self and purpose' — is a classic. (Szenthagothai, 1987, p. 324)

(1) Computers act in accordance with rules.

(2) Automatons obey rules.

(3) There are rules *represented/embodied in the brain.

The use of 'rule' would be considerably less carefree if it were appreciated that acting in accordance with a rule — as opposed to showing patterns of occurrence in accordance with certain natural laws — requires consciousness. Or if it were understood that the concept of 'implicit' rules (and unconscious rule-obedience) requires an extension of the usual sense of rule. The primary sense of a rule is of something that is inculcated and is explicitly obeyed.

We distinguish a rule from a law of nature. Although the laws of nature describe in the most general terms what happens as a rule, they are not prescriptive. As a rule, objects tend to fall downwards. This does not mean that they consciously obey the rule 'fall downwards'; or that they consult the rules in order to discover that they should fall downwards. The objects governed by the laws of nature do not try to follow that law, nor can they fail to act in accordance with it, least of all as a result of mis-understanding or misapplying it. The notion of following a rule is closely connected with that of accidentally making a mistake and of deliberate transgression. This is quite different from being subject to a (natural) law where one can hardly be mis-taken and even less in a position to flout the law.

Now it might be argued that a computer, or some other automaton, may follow the rules according to which it has been designed or programmed without 'knowing' those rules; it may exhibit rule-governed behaviour.[40] Is it not, therefore, possible to obey rules without being conscious of them, or, indeed, of anything? Well, yes, in this specially extended sense of rule-obedience, it is possible. But even here *someone* — a user, an observer — has to be conscious for the events in the automaton to be rule-obeying, for them to *count* as rule-obeying. Unless the rules are housed in a consciousness *somewhere*, the events are not rule-following.

---

[40] For a discussion of tacit rule-following (and, rather less illuminatingly, of *representation) see 'Styles of mental representation', in Dennett (1987).

One might go even further and adopt the Wittgensteinian position that rule-following is an essentially social practice, that it requires not merely one consciousness but a community of consciousnesses: 'a computer has neither inwardness nor society . . . so *it* is not following a rule.'[41] For some, this may be going too far; but it emphasises how following a rule is quite different from conforming to a natural law or exhibiting a habit or pattern of behaviour. These distinctions are rarely respected in computer-talk and other areas of cognitive psychology where rule-obedience seems to take place as well without as with consciousness.

---

[41]   Grayling (1989), p. 72.

Bibliography

Blackburn, Simon (1986), 'Finding Psychology' in *Mind, Causation and Action*, ed. Leslie Stevenson, Roger Squires and John Haldane (Oxford: Blackwell).

Blakemore, Colin (1990), *The Mind Machine* (London: BBC Books).

Blakemore, Colin and Greenfield, Susan (ed. 1987), *Mindwaves* (Oxford: Blackwell).

Boole, George (1973), *An Investigation of the Laws of Thought on Which are Founded the Mathematical Theories of Logic and Probabilities* (New York: Dover Publications).

Borst, C.V. (1970), *The Mind–Brain Identity Theory* (London: Macmillan).

Carter, Rita (1998), *Maps of the Mind* (Weidenfeld & Nicolson).

Chalmers, D.J. (1996), *The Conscious Mind: In Search of a Fundamental Theory* (New York: Oxford University Press).

Cherry, Colin (1966), *On Human Communication*, 2nd edition (Cambridge, MA: MIT Press).

Churchland, Patricia (1986), *Neurophilosophy: Towards a Unified Theory of the Mind/Brain* (Cambridge, MA: MIT Press).

Churchland, Patricia (1994), 'Can Neurobiology Teach Us Anything About Consciousness?', *Proceedings of the American Philosophical Association*, **67**, pp. 23–40.

Churchland, Paul (1988), *Matter and Consciousness*, 2nd edition (Cambridge, MA: MIT Press).

Darcy, L. and Boston, L. (1984), *A Dictionary of Computer Terms* (London: Fontana).

Davidson, Donald (1987), 'Knowing One's Own Mind', *Proceedings and Addresses of the American Philosophical Association*, **60**, pp. 441–58.

Davies, Paul (1993), *The Mind of God: Science and the Search for Ultimate Meaning* (London: Penguin).

Dawkins, Richard (1988), *The Blind Watchmaker* (London: Penguin).

Dennett, D.C. (1971), 'Intentional Systems', *Journal of Philosophy*, **8**, pp. 87–106; reprinted in *Brainstorms: Philosophical Essays on Mind and Psychology* (Montgomery, VT: Bradford Books, 1978).

Dennett, D.C. (1981), 'Three Kinds of Intentional Psychology', in *Reduction, Time and Reality*, ed. R. Healey (Cambridge: Cambridge University Press).

Dennett, D.C. (1986), 'Can machines think?', In *How We Know*, ed. M. Shafto (San Francisco: Harper and Row).

Dennett, D.C. (1987), *The Intentional Stance* (Cambridge, MA: Bradford/MIT Press).

Dennett, D.C. (1991), *Consciousness Explained* (Boston, MA: Little, Brown).

Dummett, M. (1973), *Frege: Philosophy of Language* (London: Duckworth).

Fodor, J.A. (1972), 'Some reflections on Vygotsky's "Thought and Language"', *Cognition*, 1, pp. 83–95.

Fodor, J.A. (1976), *The Language of Thought* (Brighton: Harvester Press).

Fodor, J.A. (1981), 'The Mind–Body Problem', *Scientific Amencan*, **244** (1), pp. 114–23.

Frege, Gottlob (1967), 'The Thought: A Logical Inquiry' trans. A.M. and Marcelle Quinton. Available in *Philosophical Logic (Oxford Readings in Philosophy)* ed. P.F. Strawson (Oxford: Oxford University Press).

Gellner, Ernest (1959), *Word and Object* (London, Penguin).

Grayling, A.C. (1989), *Wittgenstein* (Oxford: Oxford University Press).

Gregory, R.L. (1970), *The Intelligent Eye* (London: Weidenfeld and Nicolson).

Gregory, R.L. (1974), *Eye and Brain: the Psychology of Seeing* 3rd Edn. (London: Weidenfeld and Nicolson).

Hacker, Peter (1987), 'Languages, Minds and Brains', in Blakemore and Greenfield (1987).

Hick, W.E. (1952), 'On the rate of gain of information', *Quarterly Journal of Experimental Psychology,* 4, pp. 11–26.

Johnson-Laird, P.N. (1988), *The Computer and the Mind* (London: Fontana).

Johnson-Laird, P.N. (1983), *Mental Models: Towards a Cognitive Science of Language, Inference and Consciousness* (Cambridge: Cambridge University Press).

Kolakowski, Leszek (1972), *Positivist Philosophy: From Hume to the Vienna Circle*, trans. Norbert Guterman (London: Penguin).

Longuet-Higgins, C. (1988), 'Mental Processes', *London Review of Books*, 4th August, pp. 13–14.

McGinn, Colin (1989), 'Can we solve the mind-body problem?', *Mind*, **98** (391), pp. 349–66.

McGinn, Colin (2003), *The Making of a Philosopher* (London: Scribner).

Matthews, Eric (2002), *The Philosophy of Merleau-Ponty* (Montreal and Kingston, Ithaca: McGill Queen's).

Midgley, Mary (2002), *Science and Poetry* (London: Routledge).

Phillips, W.A. (1988), 'Brainy Minds', *Quarterly Journal of Experimental Psychology*, **40A** (2), pp. 389–405.

Pyle, Andrew (ed. 1991), *Key Philosophers in Conversation: The Cogito Interviews* (London and New York: Routledge).

Quine, W.V. (1975), 'The Nature of Natural Knowledge' in *Mind & Language*, Wolfson College Lectures 1974, ed. Samuel Guttenplan (Oxford: Clarendon Press).

Russell, James (1986), *Mental Representation and the Psychology of Knowledge* (London: Macmillan).

Ryle, G. (1949), *The Concept of Mind* (London: Hutchinson).

Searle, J.R. (1980), 'Minds, Brains, Programs', *The Behavioral and Brain Sciences*, **3**, pp. 417–57.

Searle, J.R. (1983), *Intentionality* (Cambridge: Cambridge University Press).

Searle, J.R. (1987), 'Minds and Brains without Programs', in Blakemore and Greenfield (1987).

Searle, J.R. (1997), *The Mystery of Consciousness* (London: Granta Books).

Shanker, S.G. (ed. 1986)) *Philosophy in Britain Today* (London: Croom Helm).

Shannon and Weaver (1949), *The Mathematical Theory of Communication* (Urbana: University of Illinois Press).

Spillane, J.D. (1981), *The Doctrine of the Nerves* (Oxford: Oxford University Press).

Stich, Stephen P. (1983), *From Folk Psychology to Cognitive Science: The Case Against Belief* (Cambridge, MA: MIT Press).

Stroll, Avrum (1993), 'Epistemology' in *Encyclopaedia Brittanica Macropaedia*, Vol 18, 15th Edition.

Szenthagothai, J. (1987), 'The Brain-Mind Relation: A Pseudo- Problem?', in Blakemore and Greenfield (1987).

Tallis, Raymond (1991), *The Explicit Animal: A Defence of Human Consciousness* (London: Macmillan, Second Edition, 1999).

Tallis, Raymond (1999a), *Enemies of Hope: A Critique of Contemporary Pessimism*, reprinted with new preface (London: Macmillan).

Tallis, Raymond (1999b), *On the Edge of Certainty* (London: Macmillan).

Tallis, Raymond (2000), 'Brains and Minds: A Brief History of Neuro-mythology', *Journal of Royal College of Physicians*, pp. 563–7.

Tallis, Raymond (2003), *The Hand: A Philosophical Inquiry into Human Being* (Edinburgh: Edinburgh University Press).

Tallis, Raymond (2004), *I Am: A Philosophical Inquiry into Knowledge and Truth* (Edinburgh: Edinburgh University Press).

Tallis, Raymond (2005), *The Knowing Animal: A Philosopical Inquiry into Knowledge and Truth* (Edinburgh: Edinburgh University Press).

Todorov, Tzvetan (2004), *Hope and Memory*, trans. David Bellos (London: Atlantic Books).

Toffoli, Tommaso (1982), 'Physics and Computation', *International Journal of Theoretical Physics*, **21**, pp. 160–7.

Wittgenstein, Ludwig (1953), *Philosophical Investigations* (Oxford: Blackwell).

Yates, J. (1985), 'The content of awareness is a model of the world', *Psychological Review*, **92** (2), pp. 249–84.

SOCIETAS

essays in political and cultural criticism

Contemporary public debate has been impoverished by two competing trends. On the one hand the increasing commercialization of the media has meant that in-depth commentary has given way to the ten-second soundbite. On the other hand the explosion of scholarly knowledge has led to such a degree of specialization that academic discourse has ceased to be comprehensible. As a result writing on politics and culture tends to be either superficial or baffling.

This was not always so—especially for politics. The high point of the English political pamphlet was the seventeenth century, when a number of small printer-publishers responded to the political ferment of the age with an outpouring of widely-accessible pamphlets and tracts. Indeed Imprint Academic publishes a facsimile reprints under the banner 'The Rota'.

In recent years the tradition of the political pamphlet has declined—with most publishers rejecting anything under 100,000 words. The result is that many a good idea ends up drowning in a sea of verbosity. However the digital press makes it possible to re-create a more exciting age of publishing. *Societas* authors are all experts in their own field, but the essays are for a general audience. Each book can be read in an evening.

The books are available retail at the price of £8.95/$17.90 each, or on bi-monthly subscription for only £5.00/$10.50.Full details:

www.imprint-academic.com/societas

EDITORIAL ADVISORY BOARD

IMPRINT ACADEMIC, PO Box 200, Exeter, EX5 5YX, UK
Tel: (0)1392 841600   Fax: (0)1392 841478   sandra@imprint.co.uk

SOCIETAS

essays in political and cultural criticism

Universities:
The Recovery of an Idea
Gordon Graham

The conclusion of this meditation on Cardinal Newman's *The Idea of a University* is that universities should be freed from state control.

- 'Those who care about universities should thank Gordon Graham for doing what has needed doing so urgently'. **Philosophy**
- 'Though densely and cogently argued, this book is extremely readable. **Philosophical Quarterly**

136 pp., £8.95/$17.90

Our Last Great Illusion
Rob Weatherill

Counselling and therapy yearn to bring about integration within and between people. The dominant ethos is a holistic one. This book aims to refute, primarily through the prism of modern psychoanalysis and postmodern theory, the notion of a return to nature, to holism, or to a pre-Cartesian ideal of harmony and integration. Far from helping people, therapy culture's utopian solutions may be a cynical distraction, creating delusions of hope. Yet solutions proliferate in the free market, to the precise degree that there are *no* solutions. This is why therapy is our last great illusion. Rob Weatherill lectures in psychoanalysis at Trinity College, Dublin and is a practitioner of 2years standing..

96 pp., £8.95/$17.90 0907845959

Self and Society
William Irwin Thompson

The book is comprised of a series of essays on the evolution of culture, dealing with topics including the city and consciousness, evolution of the afterlife, literary and mathematical archetypes, machine consciousness and the implications of 9/11 and the invasion of Iraq for the development of planetary culture.The author is a poet and cultural historian and the author of 16 books.

96 pp., £8.95/$17.90

sample chapters, reviews and TOCs: **www.imprint-academic.com/societas**

The Case Against the Democratic State
Gordon Graham

We are now so used to the state's pre-eminence in all things that few think to question it. This essay contends that the gross imbalance of power in the modern state is in need of justification, and that democracy simply masks this need with an illusion of popular sovereignty. Although the arguments are accessible to all, it is written within the European philosophical tradition. The author is Professor of Moral Philosophy at the Uniiversity of Aberdeen. 96 p., £8.95/$17.90

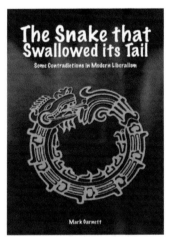

The Snake that Swallowed its Tail
Mark Garnett

Liberal values are the hallmark of a civilised society. Yet they depend on an optimistic view of the human condition, Stripped of this essential ingredient, liberalism has become a hollowed-out abstraction. Tracing its effects through the media, politics and the public services, the author argues that hollowed-out liberalism has helped to produce our present discontent. Unless we stop boasting about our values and try to recover their essence, liberal society will be crushed in the coils of its own contradictions. 96 pp., £8.95/$17.90

The Party's Over
Keith Sutherland

The book argues that the tyranny of the modern political party should be replaced by a mixed constitution in which advocacy is entrusted to an aristocracy of merit, and democratic representation is achieved via a jury-style lottery. 200 pp., £8.95/$17.90

- *'An extremely valuable contribution–a subversive and necessary read.'* **Graham Allen MP**, *Tribune*
- *'His analysis of what is wrong is superb . . . No one can read this book without realising that something radical, even revolutionary must be done.'* **Sir Richard Body**, *Salisbury Review*

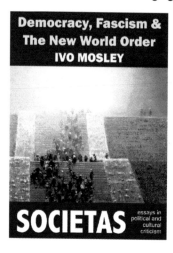

Democracy, Fascism and the New World Order
Ivo Mosley

Growing up as the grandson of the 1930s blackshirt leader, made Ivo Mosley consider fascism with a deep interest. Whereas conventional wisdom sets up democracy and fascism as opposites, to ancient political theorists democracy had an innate tendency to lead to extreme populist government, and provided demagogues with the opportunity to seize power. This book argues that totalitarian regimes can be the outcome of unfettered mass democracy. 96 pp., £8.95/$17.90

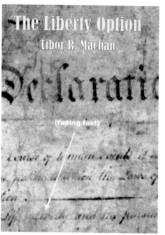

The Liberty Option
Tibor R. Machan

This book advances the idea that for compelling moral and practical reasons it is the society organised on classical liberal principles that serves justice best, leads to prosperity and encourages the greatest measure of individual virtue. The book contrasts the Lockean ideal with the various statist alternatives, defends it against its communitarian critics and lays out some of its policy implications. Machan is a research fellow at Stanford University. His books include *Classical Individualism* (Routledge, 1998). 104 pp., £8.95/$17.90

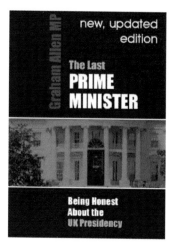

The Last Prime Minister
Graham Allen MP

Echoing Gandhi, Graham Allen thinks the British constitution would be a very good idea. In *The Last Prime Minister* he showed the British people how they had acquired an executive presidency by stealth. This timely new edition takes in new issues, including Parliament's constitutional impotence over Iraq.

'Well-informed and truly alarming.' **Peter Hennessy**

'Iconoclastic, and well-argued, it's publication could hardly be more timely.' **Vernon Bogdanor, THES**

96 pp. £8.95/$17.90

sample chapters, reviews and TOCs: **www.imprint-academic.com/societas**